UNIVERSITY OF
GLOUCESTERSHIRE

NORMAL LOAN

DORIS LESSING

Doris
Lessing

Elizabeth Maslen

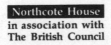

Northcote House
in association with
The British Council

WRITERS AND THEIR WORK
Series Editors:
ISOBEL ARMSTRONG AND BRYAN LOUGHREY

First published in 1994 by Northcote House Publishers Ltd,
Plymbridge House, Estover Road, Plymouth PL6 7PZ,
United Kingdom.
Tel: Plymouth (0752) 735251. Fax: (0752) 695699. Telex: 45635.

British Library Cataloguing-in-Publication Data
A catalogue record for this book is available from the British Library

ISBN 0 7463 0705 5

Typeset by Kestrel Data, Exeter
Printed and bound in Great Britain by BPCC Wheatons Ltd, Exeter.

Contents

Acknowledgements

Some of the discussion of Doris Lessing's novels first appeared in two articles of mine in the *Doris Lessing Newsletter*: 'Doris Lessing: The Way to Space Fiction' (spring, 1984), and 'Narrators and Readers in Three Novels' (fall, 1986).

The author and the publishers are grateful to the following for permission to reproduce copyright material as follows:

'The Asia Article', copyright © by Doris Lessing. Reprinted by permission of Jonathan Clowes Ltd., London, on behalf of Doris Lessing; *The Summer before the Dark*, copyright © 1973 the Doris Lessing Trust. Reprinted by permission of Jonathan Clowes Ltd., London, on behalf of the Doris Lessing Trust; *The Diary of a Good Neighbour*, copyright © 1983 Doris Lessing/Jane Somers. Reprinted by permission of Jonathan Clowes Ltd., London, on behalf of Doris Lessing; 'The Old Chief Mshlanga' (short story), copyright © 1951 Doris Lessing. Reprinted by permission of Jonathan Clowes Ltd., London, on behalf of Doris Lessing; 'The Sun between their Feet' (short story), copyright © 1963 Doris Lessing. Reprinted by permission of Jonathan Clowes Ltd., London, on behalf of Doris Lessing; 'Debbie & Julie' (short story), copyright © 1988 Doris Lessing. Reprinted by permission of Jonathan Clowes Ltd., London, on behalf of Doris Lessing; 'Principles' (short story), copyright 1988 Doris Lessing. Reprinted by permission of Jonathan Clowes Ltd, London, on behalf of Doris Lessing; 'Impertinent Daughters', copyright © 1984, 1985 Doris Lessing. Reprinted by permission of Jonathan Clowes Ltd., London, on behalf of Doris Lessing; *The Wind Blows away our Words*, copyright © 1987 Doris Lessing. Reprinted by permission of Jonathan Clowes Ltd., London, on behalf of Doris Lessing; Article from *Partisan Review*: fall 1992 – untitled article for Conference on Intellectual and Social change in central and eastern Europe pp. 722-30, copyright © 1992 Doris Lessing. Reprinted by permission of Jonathan Clowes Ltd., London, on behalf of Doris Lessing.

Biographical Plan

1919	Born in Persia (Iran) of British parents.
1925	Moved with parents to farm in Southern Rhodesia.
1938	Joined left-wing group which, during the war, gave rise to more organized Marxist group.
1939	Married civil servant, Frank Wisdom. Two children, John and Jean.
1943	Divorced.
1945	Married Gottfried Lessing, refugee from Nazi Germany.
1947	Son, Peter, born.
1949	Divorced. Came to England with son and with manuscript of *The Grass is Singing*.
1950	First novel, *The Grass is Singing*, published in England.
1952	Visited Soviet Union.
1952–3	Assisted Margot Heinemann in editing *Daylight*, magazine for working-class writers.
1956	Resigned from Communist Party. Declared prohibited immigrant by Southern Rhodesia and barred from entry into South Africa.
1958	Helped to organize first CND march.
1962	*The Golden Notebook* published.
1969	*The Four-Gated City* published.
1974	*Memoirs of a Survivor* published; made into a film in 1981.
1983	Published *The Diary of a Good Neighbour* under pseudonym 'Jane Somers'.
1985	*The Good Terrorist* nominated for Booker Prize and won the W. H. Smith award.
1992	*African Laughter* published.

Abbreviations and References

AL	*African Laughter* (London: HarperCollins, 1992)
BDH	*Briefing for a Descent into Hell* (London: Grafton, 1972)
CAS	*Collected African Stories* (London: Collins (Paladin), 1992)
CP	*Re: Colonised Planet 5, Shikasta* (London: Grafton, 1981)
DGN	*The Diary of a Good Neighbour* (London: Joseph, 1983)
DLR	*The Doris Lessing Reader* (London: Collins (Paladin), 1991)
FC	*The Fifth Child* (London: Collins (Paladin), 1989)
FGC	*The Four-Gated City* (London: Collins (Paladin), 1990)
GH	*Going Home* (London: HarperCollins (Flamingo), 1992)
GN	*The Golden Notebook* (London: Collins (Paladin), 1989)
GS	*The Grass is Singing* (London: Collins (Paladin), 1989)
GT	*The Good Terrorist* (London: Collins (Paladin), 1990)
ID	'Impertinent Daughters', *Granta*, Cambridge, 14 (winter, 1984)
L.	*Landlocked* (London: Collins (Paladin), 1990)
LO	*London Observed: Stories and Sketches* (London: HarperCollins, 1992)
MQ	*Martha Quest* (London: Collins (Paladin), 1990)
MRP	*The Making of the Representative for Planet 8* (London: Grafton, 1983)
MS	*The Memoirs of a Survivor* (London: Pan (Picador), 1976)
MTW	*A Man and Two Women* (London: Collins (Paladin), 1992)
MZ	*The Marriages between Zones Three, Four and Five* (London: Grafton, 1981)
PE	*In Pursuit of the English* (London: HarperCollins (Flamingo), 1993)

PM	*A Proper Marriage* (London: Collins (Paladin), 1990)
RS	*A Ripple from the Storm* (London: Collins (Paladin), 1990)
SA	*Documents Relating to the Sentimental Agents in the Volyen Empire* (London: Grafton, 1985)
SD	*The Summer before the Dark* (London: Collins (Paladin), 1990)
WBW	*The Wind Blows away our Words* (London: Pan (Picador), 1987)
UMA	'Unexamined Mental Attitudes Left Behind by Communism', *Partisan Review*, Special Issue (fall, 1992), 722–30
Bakhtin	*The Dialogic Imagination: Four Essays by M. M. Bakhtin*, ed M. Holquist, trans. C. Emerson and M. Holquist (Austin: University of Texas Press, 1981)
Foucault	*The Foucault Reader*, ed. P. Rabinow (London: Penguin, 1984)
Greene	G. Greene, *Changing the Story: Feminist Fiction and the Tradition* (Bloomington, Ind.: Indiana University Press, 1991)

1

Introduction

It is not easy to know where to begin when discussing Doris Lessing's works, as they cover such a range of ideas and experience. She is always engaged with the world of Now, wrestling not only with those matters which are central debates of the moment at which she writes, but also with issues which ought to be debated, but which the society she writes for is not quite ready to face. So in the early 1950s she confronted racism and exposed its language of coded words and silences in, for instance, *The Grass is Singing*; in the early 1960s she explored issues ranging from women's engagement with matters of gender to mental breakdown in *The Golden Notebook*; in the 1970s she wrote about the importance of coming to terms with inner space in *Briefing for a Descent into Hell* and *The Memoirs of a Survivor*; in the 1980s she probed both the human and inhuman face of terrorism in *The Good Terrorist*. And these are a random selection of what she engages with in her work.

Nor does she always write the same kind of novel; she is constantly testing fresh ways of communicating with her readers. She frequently moves from telling stories in chronological sequence, with linear narrative, to different kinds of layered novel, whether confronting 'fact', fiction, and points of view in the sectionalized notebooks of *The Golden Notebook*, or alternating views of the life of the mind and what goes on in the outside world, which we find in *Briefing for a Descent into Hell* and *The Memoirs of a Survivor*. Then again there is the space fiction reporting of an alien official in *Re: Colonised Planet 5, Shikasta* and the fabular narrative of *The Marriages between Zones Three, Four and Five*; and there is the realism of *The Good Terrorist* and *The Fifth Child*.

Throughout her work, Doris Lessing is always aware of the power and complexity of language. M. M. Bakhtin, in his 'Discourse in the Novel', argues how,

1

the novel can be defined as a diversity of social speech types . . . and a diversity of individual voices, artistically organized. The internal stratification of any single national language into social dialects, characteristic group behavior, professional jargons, generic languages, languages of generations and age groups, tendentious languages, languages of the authorities, of various circles and of passing fashions, languages that serve the specific sociopolitical purposes of the day, even of the hour (each day has its own slogan, its own vocabulary, its own emphases) – this internal stratification present in every language at any given moment of its historical existence is the indispensable prerequisite for the novel as a genre. (Bakhtin, 262–3)

Doris Lessing has a keen ear for this 'internal stratification' and she represents individual voices, entering into all kinds of relations with them through irony and parody. She is also keenly aware of how each individual has access to many language systems, each for different contexts, sometimes intentionally, sometimes intuitively, like the nineteenth-century Russian peasant Bakhtin describes, who

prayed to God in one language (Church Slavonic), sang songs in another, spoke to his family in a third and, when he began to dictate petitions to the local authorities through a scribe, he tried speaking yet a fourth language (the official-literate language, 'proper' language) . . . he passed from one to the other without thinking, automatically: each was indisputably in its own place, and the place of each was indisputable . . . as soon as it became clear that these were not only various different languages but . . . that the ideological systems and approaches to the world that were indissolubly connected with these languages contradicted each other and in no way could live in peace and quiet with one another – then the inviolability and predetermined quality of these languages came to an end, and the necessity of actively choosing one's orientation among them began. (Bakhtin, 295–6)

Doris Lessing excels at showing such moments of crisis; *The Golden Notebook*, for instance, among many other such awakenings, shows Anna and Molly realizing the emptiness of a political jargon previously taken for granted. Doris Lessing demonstrates how all kinds of issues infect words (political loyalties, for example, or the films we watch, or the generally unspoken conventions of the particular section of society in which we live). She is remarkably clever at placing different languages in situations where we can hear their differences clearly and, as it were, listen to the debate and draw our own conclusions. She is, as I hope to show, one of the most wide-ranging and challenging explorers of the contemporary world, and her understanding of what language does to us as well as for us would be difficult to overestimate.

2

Publications of the 1950s

Doris Lessing's first novel, *The Grass is Singing* (1950), is set in Southern Rhodesia (now Zimbabwe) where she grew up. It tells the story of a white woman, Mary, who leaves the poor family farm on the veld to live a happy single life in the town until she feels pushed by her friends into seeking a husband. Disastrously, she marries Dick Turner, a poor and stubborn farmer, and, in the frustrations of a life mirroring her own mother's, gradually deteriorates into breakdown, and in so doing crosses a taboo line: from despising and hating 'natives' in the way conventional within her own cultural context, she comes to rely physically and emotionally on her black servant, Moses. When Tony, a young man fresh from England, arrives on the farm, she sends Moses away, only to have him return and kill her.

A bald summary of the plot gives no sign of the skill Doris Lessing demonstrates in weaving together the languages of her novel. For instance, Mary's early life in town, after her escape from her parents' farm, is described as 'very happy' and the conventions of that life are built up in terms of routine:

> Her voice was one of thousands: flattened, a little sing-song, clipped. Anyone could have worn her clothes . . . she played tennis, or hockey, or swam. And always with a man, one of those innumerable men, who 'took her out', treating her like a sister: Mary was such a good pal! . . . And in the evening she always went to sundowner parties . . . she was never in bed before twelve or later. And so it had gone on, day after day, week after week, year after year. (*GS* 36-8)

But the language of conformity reminds us that it is also a language of surfaces; we are told that 'she *seemed* impersonal, above the little worries . . . she *seemed* immune' (*GS* 37; emphasis added). The language at this stage does not show anything of Mary's inner life. At the same time, the routine of her life is not offered uncritically;

4

we are told her 'full and active life' was 'a passive one, in some respects, for it depended on other people entirely' (*GS* 37). Such dependence will be recalled later, in the loneliness of the farm, where she becomes utterly dependent on Moses and where, once she has banished him, she looks to the young Englishman to 'save' her. Her 'happy' life in town ends because 'she was not playing her part, for she did not get married' (*GS* 38), and she responds to the implied criticism by conforming, by marrying; yet on the farm, when she tries to lead a 'full and active life' helping Dick, she encounters his obstinacy and gradually fades into what has to become a regressive alternative, passive dependence on Moses, so that, when Tony hears her telling Moses to 'Go away', he hears that 'she was speaking like a child challenging a grown-up person' (*GS* 188). She is, as it were, back on the farm of her childhood, challenging her father.

The different languages that Bakhtin refers to are clearly evident throughout. For instance, towards the end of the novel, as Mary, in the grip of breakdown, waits in terror for Moses, she thinks of the 'youth', the young Englishman, and the language of her fear clashes with the comforting clichés drawn from the films and magazines of her years in town:

> He had been kind to her; he had not condemned her. Suddenly she found herself clinging to the thought of him. He would save her. She would wait for him to return. She stood in the doorway looking down over the sweep of sere, dry vlei. Somewhere in the trees *he* was waiting; somewhere in the vlei was the young man, who would come before the night to rescue her. She stared, hardly blinking, into the aching sunlight. But what was the matter with the big land down there, which was always an expanse of dull red at this time of the year! It was covered over with bushes and grass. Panic plucked at her; already, before she was even dead, the bush was conquering the farm, sending its outriders to cover the good red soil with plants and grass; the bush knew she was going to die! But the young man . . . shutting out everything else she thought of him, with his warm comfort, his protecting arm. (*GS* 198)

Bakhtin asserts that one of the great strengths of the novel genre is that it embraces heteroglossia, invasions from the culture, the society in which particular novels are written. Michel Foucault (in *Discipline and Punish*, for example) shows how a society establishes discourses of power, discourses (not necessarily expressed in words) which have ways of compelling us to subscribe to their priorities, spoken or unspoken. Doris Lessing is very alert to such discourses, as has already been demonstrated by Mary's passive conformity to the conventions of town life and by the way in which she transfers her need for a strong man, born of that conformity, first and fatally to Moses, and then to the hero of film or story, the young man who, she fantasizes, will save her. Her tragedy is that her need for a conventional dependence on a man takes her into territory which is utterly outside the then dominant discourse of white, Southern Rhodesian society. This is powerfully illustrated in the opening chapters of the novel, where the white sergeant of police and the prosperous, neighbouring farmer, Charlie Slatter, confront the new arrival from England, Tony, after Mary's murder (for the novel begins with the aftermath of the murder and then goes back over her life and death). Tony is gradually made aware that, when they question him about what happened, he is in fact being wordlessly coached into certain responses. They are not really seeking the truth, but Tony's acceptance of the rules of their society. Mary's image as white woman murdered by native must be untarnished and un-complicated; her (for them) unforgivable closeness with that native must be obliterated. Tony senses he is under pressure yet, despite his anger and frustration, is helpless against this pressure. Doris Lessing leaves us in no doubt that he is confronting the dominant discourse of this society, for Charlie Slatter enters the novel as a type ('he . . . personified Society for the Turners' (*GS* 13)), and in turn he typecasts the young man Tony (Slatter 'knew the type so well' (*GS* 17)). And then a narrative voice gives us a clear lesson in how to translate the mere words of Slatter and the sergeant: 'When old settlers say "One has to understand the country," what they mean is, "You have to get used to our ideas about the native". They are saying, in effect, "Learn our ideas, or otherwise get out: we don't want you" ' (*GS* 18). The discourse this passage reveals is reminiscent of Orwell's Thought Police in *Nineteen Eighty-Four* and Doris Lessing invites us to go beyond the covers of her book, in Bakhtin's way, in Foucault's way, by giving us as one of the epigraphs for the book: 'It is by the failures and misfits of a civilization that one can best judge its weaknesses' (author unknown).

I have spent some time on *The Grass is Singing* because it is a fine novel in its own right and because it demonstrates so many of the skills that pervade Doris Lessing's works. Her refusal to turn away from what society rejects and attempts to ignore is typical of her; she has a capacity to see and hear more clearly than most what is going on. And, as her writing continues, she will go further, drawing conclusions from the tendencies she observes and predicting imaginatively where such tendencies may lead. It is this formidable capacity to extrapolate from the present into the future which gives her the air of being a seer; she is not confined in her writing by what has gone before or by what is happening now. She shows the links between what a Marxist dreams of, the concerns of the spiritual seeker, and the vision of the science-fiction writer, for she will never let us forget that what we do now will affect what happens in the future. Cause and effect have always been matters of concern for story-tellers, for novelists, of course; but the causes are usually past, their effects in the present or in the more recent past. Doris Lessing is not afraid to go a stage further.

Her next venture was to begin what would become a sequence of five novels, The Children of Violence, popularly known as the 'Martha Quest' books. This sequence was to be published over the next seventeen years, and would change dramatically in that time from the story of Martha's life to an apocalyptic look at where society is heading. In its development it shows another of Doris Lessing's qualities as a writer. Because, while the sequence grows and changes, there are striking threads of continuity. Her work may be described in the words Ted Hughes used when describing the poems of the Serbian poet, Vasko Popa, in the preface to Popa's Collected Poems, 1943–76:

> One begins to feel the large consistent wholeness behind the swarming parts . . . They smoulder along through years, criss-crossing each other, keeping the character of their own genes, working out their completeness. Until the cycles themselves, which are already made up of smaller cycles, begin to look like members of greater cycles . . . it begins to look like a Universe passing through a Universe.

For instance, in the first volume of the sequence, Martha Quest (1952), Doris Lessing introduces the adolescent Martha having a vision of a city on the veld:

> and its citizens moved, grave and beautiful, black and white and brown together; and these groups of elders paused, and smiled with pleasure at the sight of the children – the blue-eyed, fair-skinned children of the North playing hand in hand with the bronze-skinned, dark-eyed children of the South. Yes, they smiled and approved these many-fathered children, running and playing among the flowers and the terraces,

through the white pillars and tall trees of this fabulous and ancient city
. . . (MQ 21)

This vision, offered to us in the language of Martha's as yet book-led mind, will be reviewed in the third novel of the sequence, *A Ripple from the Storm* (1958), as a future promised by Communism; eleven years later it will be reassessed with fresh psychological insights in the final volume of the sequence, *The Four-Gated City* (1969), and will be explored again in the first volume of the Canopus in Argos: Archives sequence in 1979. Each exploration will add to the original idea of the city, drawing on discourses of a society beyond the confines of the novels, but none will actually negate the original moment when Martha has her vision on the veld.

Another example of a continuing vision occurs first in *A Proper Marriage*, the second book of Children of Violence, when Martha looks at her mother and sees, with a prophetic insight that she learns to combat,

a sequence of events, unalterable, behind her, and stretching unalterably into the future. She saw her mother, a prim-faced Edwardian schoolgirl, confronting, in this case, the Victorian father, the patriarchal father, with rebellion. She saw herself sitting where her mother now sat, a woman horribly metamorphosed, entirely dependent on her children for any interest in life, resented by them, and resenting them; opposite her, a young woman of whom she could distinguish nothing clearly but a set, obstinate face; and beside these women, a series of shadowy dependent men, broken-willed and sick with compelled diseases. This is the nightmare, this the nightmare of a class and generation: repetition. (*PM* 126)

In *A Proper Marriage* this vision of a destructive discourse of women in family heralds protest and rebellion; twenty years later, in *The Memoirs of a Survivor*, it is reviewed and finally contained within a larger, optimistic discourse, as the protagonist of this later novel learns how to explore her inner life and to understand her heritage more clearly, the pattern being not so much broken as rewoven into a hope for the future.

And this is true also of the handling of the 'poor-farm' material in *Martha Quest*, which has much in common with the poor farm in *The Grass is Singing*. Here again we have the husband who is a dreamer rather than a practical farmer, and the wife who is ruled by the conventions of a gentility which is at odds with the confines and failure of the farm. But in *Martha Quest* the couple are Martha's parents, and Martha, unlike the Mary of *The Grass is Singing*, is an active shaper of her own destiny. Later, *A Proper Marriage*, like *The Grass is Singing*, explores the social pressures on a woman both to marry and to maintain a certain role within marriage, only this time from the point of view of the highly intelligent Martha, who can hear and analyse the difference between society's powerfully persuasive discourse and her own small questioning inner voice, and who is capable of sustaining, albeit painfully, a dialogue between the two. These books are intriguingly and fruitfully related, and are indeed precursors of aspects of *The Golden Notebook* (1962), since all of these novels are concerned with ways in which society's expectations and personal aspirations are perilously polarized in the lives of the main characters, compartmentalized in ways which are explored and exposed as the enemies of fulfilment in *The Golden Notebook*. Doris Lessing has an impressive capacity for reworking the same raw material in different, mutually enlightening ways. She affirms in her writing that the fictionalizing of fact, the privileging of fiction over fact, can in many cases be closer to truth than what is recorded as history, and in this she is interestingly in accord with the postmodern attitudes to history, represented, for example, in the works of Julian Barnes or Graham Swift.

I think it important to note this ability at the outset of Doris Lessing's career as a writer, since the Children of Violence books are both a contribution to and a formidable extension of what she herself has termed (in her afterword to *The Four-Gated City*) a *Bildungsroman*, that is to say, what can be defined as the story of a life. For, while Martha's life is indeed charted from beginning to end, Doris Lessing is not trapped by the expectations aroused by this label for a specific kind of novel-writing: her move from a world which we recognize from shared experience to a world where Martha exerts communal skills (described in terms of telepathy) to nurture a new breed of humans (one of whom is classed as mentally retarded according to conventional educational assessment, while having alternative, evolved powers never before tapped) – such a move reinvents the concept of *Bildungsroman* and challenges the reader to reassess what development, both personal and communal, can mean.

And it is exciting to see the way in which issues which will be explored later, not just in The Children of Violence but in *The Golden Notebook* and throughout Doris Lessing's work, have their roots in these early novels. Most obviously, in the first two novels of the sequence, as in *The Grass is Singing*, she is addressing the plight of women and how it is shaped and maintained by society's discourses. In all three novels we see male fantasy at work, with poor Dick's idealized image of the perfect girl obscuring Mary in the earlier work, while Martha is more aggressively manipulated by the men she meets: the wolves of the Sports Club with their endlessly sterile sexual teasing; Donovan with his dressing and shaping of her so as to make her literally conform to his idea of what her image should be; Adolf, himself trapped by prejudice and paranoia, with his lessons on how to use and abuse; and Douglas, at first the means for an easy capitulation to the discourse of convention but, when Martha's personal integrity sets up a dialogue with this convention, a histrionic sadist bent on forcing Martha, like Mary, to 'play her part'.

In all three novels, however, Doris Lessing also shows women as active manipulators of other women: Mary's move from the single status she happily enjoys into a disastrous marriage is caused by the good-humoured malice of overheard women's talk, while Martha's adolescence and marriage are a continual battle against her mother's expectation of her and crude invasions of her private space. All three novels also show the effects of the written word on women: the non-intellectual Mary succumbs to what the magazines which she reads (which are supported by the films she sees) require of her, while Martha, the voracious reader, constantly debates the strengths and limitations of the books she reads to deal with what she is experiencing as a girl-woman. She sees herself 'in the only way she was equipped to do this' (*MQ* 17) through the literature she has read. She is surprised at its silence on the pains of growing up and, since she does not yet possess the vocabulary to accuse it for its silences, concludes that 'if novels accurately reflect, as we hope and trust they do, the life of their era, then one is forced to conclude that being young was much easier then that it is now, (*MQ* 17). A little later in Salisbury she is more certain about what is not relevant for her as a woman: 'And so these authors, these philosophers who had fed and maintained (or so she understood) so many earlier generations, were discarded with the ease with which she had shed religion: they wouldn't do, or not for her' (*MQ* 272).

Or again, in *A Proper Marriage*, she ponders (always in dialogue with the literature she loves):

Or do you suppose they didn't tell the truth, the novelists? In the books, the young and idealistic girl gets married, has a baby – she at once turns into something quite different; and she is perfectly happy to spend her whole life bringing up children with a tedious husband. Natasha, for instance [in *War and Peace*]: she was content to be an old hen, fussing and dull; but supposing all the time she saw a picture of herself as she had been, and saw herself as what she had become and was miserable – what then? Because either that's the truth or there is a completely new kind of woman in the world, and surely that isn't possible . . . (*PM* 268)

Here we are presented with a Martha aware of the difference between the language of girlhood and the language of marriage; she spots the shift from one of these languages to the other in Natasha (as in Bakhtin's description of the Russian peasant's shifts between his four languages), while she herself, Martha, is *aware* of her own shift of language and, being aware, has noted the contradictions between them and so has to choose her orientation.

Earlier, in *Martha Quest*, she wrestles in passing with problems that will be more fully debated in *The Golden Notebook* – such as the helplessness of writers to change what they deplore. So, for instance, as she sees a line of chained black men and women being taken off to the magistrate, she thinks desperately:

It's all so dreadful, not because it exists, merely, but because it exists *now*. She was thinking – for, since she had been formed by literature, she could think in no other way – that all this had been described in Dickens, Tolstoy, Hugo, Dostoevsky, and a dozen others. All that noble and terrific indignation had done nothing, achieved nothing, the shout of anger from the nineteenth century might as well have been silent . . . (*MQ* 226)

And yet Martha has been wakened to the injustices by what she has read as well as by experience, and Doris Lessing, like her own Anna Wulf in *The Golden Notebook*, goes on writing about the oppression of society's discourses, holding a dialogue with them, devising different ways of presenting them, so that her readers cannot retreat into the kind of recognition which allows them to choose to look away.

The issue of race which Martha confronts in the passage quoted above broods over all the works preceding *The Golden Notebook*, if in very different ways. In *The Grass is Singing* it emerges in profoundly personal terms within a framework of a cultural silence represented by Charlie Slatter and the police sergeant, with Doris Lessing probing the kind of mind which initially succumbs to conformism but, when isolated from the society which made the rules, is mesmerized by the otherness which conformism rejects because it fears. Violence ends the uneasy bonding between the black Moses and the white Mary, destroying both in an end to a forbidden dialogue. In *Martha Quest* racism extends to cover the distrust of Jews, the growing hostility between Afrikaner and English, as well as the racism based on colour. And the awareness of such injustices in *Martha Quest* goes hand in hand with Martha's wavering but none the less increasing interest in socialism, which will develop in *A Proper Marriage* and the next book in the sequence, *A Ripple from the Storm*, into an exploration of Marxism and a fuller exploration of the colour question.

In *A Ripple from the Storm* the 'Martha Quest' books change in emphasis, as this is much more a novel of ideas, a novel about social ideologies, than an exploration of Martha's growing consciousness as a woman, although that is by no means lost sight of. For instance, now divorced from Douglas, she reflects on a conventional depiction of woman as lost without her mate (anticipating one of the central issues debated in *The Golden Notebook*), ironically exploring the language of the romantic novel of the period:

> There is a type of woman who can never be, as they are likely to put it 'themselves', with anyone but the man to whom they have permanently or not given their hearts. If the man goes away there is left an empty space filled with shadows. She mourns for the temporarily extinct person she can only be with a man she loves; she mourns him who brought her 'self' to life. She lives with the empty space at her side, peopled with the images of her own potentialities until the next man walks into the space, absorbs the shadows into himself, creating her, allowing her to be her 'self' – but a new self, since it is his conception which forms her. (*RS* 54–5)

But much of *A Ripple from the Storm* is taken up with detailed accounts of the meetings and internal wranglings of the Communist group Martha belongs to. The way in which these concerns and quarrels are recorded is often parodic, their naïveties often treated ironically, a development which is not so surprising when we recall that the novel was published in 1958, after Doris Lessing had left the Communist Party in the wake of Krushchev's betrayal of his own liberalizing statements by the invasion of Hungary in 1956. The irony is very evident, for instance, in this passage, with its image of the visionary city first found in *Martha Quest*:

> A small ragged, barefooted black child, pot-bellied with malnutrition, hesitated on the opposite corner . . . Martha and Jasmine smiled at each other, saying in the smile that because of them, because of their vision, he was protected and saved: the future they dreamed of seemed just around the corner; they could almost touch it. Each saw an ideal town, clean, noble and beautiful, soaring up over the actual town they saw, which consisted in this area of sordid little shops and third-rate cafés. The ragged child was already a citizen of this ideal town, co-citizen with themselves; they watched him out of sight around the corner smiling: it was as if they had touched him with their hands in friendship. (*RS* 40)

In this passage the clash of Bakhtinian languages, where the girls 'choose' their vision, as it were, instead of the reality of the sordid street, exposes a flaw in those adherents of ideologies who pitch their tents in the future at the expense of the present. None the less a passage in *The Golden Notebook* shows an irony which is relevant to *A Ripple from the Storm*. Here, Anna Wulf (the protagonist of *The Golden Notebook*) analyses what the existence of a Communist Party prompted in 'our small town' in Africa (very like the Salisbury of Martha Quest):

> In our own small town, a year after Russia entered the war, and the left had recovered because of it, there had come into existence (apart from the direct activities of the party which is not what I am talking about) a small orchestra, readers' circles, two dramatic groups, a film society, an amateur survey of the conditions of urban African children which, when it was published, stirred the white conscience and was the beginning of a long-over-due sense of guilt, and half a dozen discussion groups on African problems. For the first time in its existence there was something like a cultural life in that town. And it was enjoyed by hundreds of people who knew of the communists only as a group of people to hate. And of course a good many of these phenomena were disapproved of by the communists themselves . . . Yet the communists had inspired them because a dedicated faith in humanity *spreads ripples* in all directions. (*GN* 79–80; emphasis added)

A Ripple from the Storm does indeed show something of what Anna Wulf describes in the later novel. But it is intriguing to compare this Martha Quest book with the non-fiction work which Doris Lessing had produced the year before in 1957, *Going Home*. In *Going Home* her point of view is actually situated in 1956, whereas in *A Ripple from the Storm* the perspective is ostensibly situated at the time described in the novel, that is, during the Second World War, when Martha herself (and Doris Lessing) was a committed member of the Communist group. As a result, the voice in the novel which describes Communist meetings and ideas with a certain sense of ironic absurdity seems to reflect a narrative viewpoint of 1958 rather than of the time in question. Of course we are accustomed to the intelligent reactions and comments which are a part of the developing Martha, but in *A Ripple from the Storm*, the ironizing language does not come solely from Martha herself, either in conversation or thought, but is woven into the narrative. However, as *Going Home* is situated in 1956, its narrative voices are situated in the book's own time and the narrator is presented to us as the author, reassessing the situation in Southern Rhodesia and the Central African Federation as a whole with astuteness and humour, while interlacing with comment on politics and the atrocities emanating from an increasingly brutal imposition of the colour bar moments of sensitively conveyed nostalgia, personal reminiscence, and those startling, graphically visual evocations of veld and vlei which Doris Lessing always does so well.

Among other things in *Going Home*, she discusses the role of the writer in ways which throw light on a whole range of her work. She says, for instance:

> After all, I said, I could hardly be called a politically active person. For the business of earning one's living by writing does not leave much time for politics; and in any case, it is one of my firmest principles that a writer should not become involved in day-to-day politics . . . But I do not stick to this principle. For one thing, my puritan sense of duty which nothing can suppress is always driving me out to meetings which I know are a waste of time, let alone those meetings which are useful but which would be better assisted by someone else; for another, I find political behaviour inexhaustibly fascinating. Nevertheless, I am not a political agitator. I am an agitator *manquée*. I sublimate this side of my personality by mixing with people who are. (*GH* 49–50)

These comments relate back to the reflections on writing and action found in *Martha Quest*, and also offer some insight into why Doris Lessing so consistently deplores the tendency of critics to try to 'label' her. And it is interesting to set the above passage against this next comment: 'But it was not that I wanted to be a journalist, I said; I had to be one, in order to pay my expenses. And besides it would be good for me to be a journalist for a time, a person collecting facts and information, after being a novelist, *who has to go inwards to probe out the truth'* (*GH* 50; emphasis added). This distinction is an intriguing one, especially as Doris Lessing so consistently addresses problematic issues relevant to the moments about which she is writing in her novels. The important point here, I think, is her feeling that the anchorage for fiction is within, as the probing of inner space will be an increasingly important preoccupation of subsequent novels. However, she never regrets her affiliations with the Communists. Eleven years after writing *Going Home*, she wrote an endnote (called in subsequent editions 'Eleven Years Later') to the book and among other things explained what for her had been important about the Communist Party in Southern Rhodesia, saying: 'But when you joined the Communists you met, for the first time, people of other races, and on equal terms. It was for this reason the Communist party had influence: not because of its theories' (*GH* 248). And she also says:

> And I'm grateful to the Communists for what they taught me: particularly about power, the realities of political power. It is no accident that the only group of people who knew the Federation [i.e. of Northern and Southern Rhodesia and Nyasaland – now Zambia, Zimbabwe and Malawi] was dangerous nonsense, that Partnership [i.e. limited votes for non-whites] was a bad joke, were Socialists of various kinds. (*GH* 247)

In a still later edition (1982) she added a further afterword, 'Twenty-Six Years Later', pointing to some things in *Going Home* which she now considered blind spots and adding:

> Looking back, I say to myself that ideally I would like to have been a communist for let's say two years, because of what I learned about the nature of power, power-lovers, fanatics, the dynamics of groups and how they form and split, about one's own capacity for self-delusion. Of course this is impossible. I am wondering if there is some psychological law that dictates the length of time it takes to recover from the effects of a submission away from commonsense, to a faith, whether political or religious. There must be stages of this, like an illness; a slow recovery from absolutism, through degrees of agnosticism. (*GH* 253–4)

It is not for nothing that, in all her writings, Doris Lessing demonstrates such a keen understanding of what Michel Foucault identifies as discourses of power, and indeed her debt to Marxism is profound, as Gayle Greene points out in the brilliant chapter on *The Golden Notebook* in her book, *Changing the Story: Feminist Fiction and the Tradition* (1991):

> Lessing was drawn to Marxist aesthetics because it was concerned with questions that concerned her – about the ideological complicity of language and convention, the relationship of politics to art, the possibility of revolutionary form. (Greene, 115)

3

The Golden Notebook and the End of Martha Quest

Going Home both marks a break in the Children of Violence sequence and does not, as it throws so much light on Doris Lessing's other writing at this point and deals with so many of the issues that are preoccupying her in *A Ripple from the Storm*. And this sense of interruption which at the same time blends in with the 'Martha Quest' books is even more marked with the publication in 1962 of her next novel, *The Golden Notebook*.

It is hard to give an impression of the richness of *The Golden Notebook* in a few sentences. Doris Lessing broke off the 'Martha Quest' series to attempt a work on a far larger scale, encompassing a wide-ranging engagement with contemporary society seen through the eyes of women. In the preface which she added nine years later, Doris Lessing describes the shape of the novel:

> There is a skeleton, or frame, called *Free Women*, which is a conventional short novel, about 60,000 words long, and which could stand by itself. But it is divided into five sections and separated by stages of the four Notebooks, Black, Red, Yellow and Blue. The Notebooks are kept by Anna Wulf, a central character of *Free Women*. She keeps four, and not one because, as she recognizes, she has to separate things off from each other, out of fear of chaos, of formlessness – of breakdown. Pressures, inner and outer, end the Notebooks; a heavy black line is drawn across the page of one after another. But now that they are finished can come something new, *The Golden Notebook*. (GN 7)

Doris Lessing explores the 'patterns and formulas' we make 'to shore up' ourselves, and shows how such compartmentalizing falsifies, as she exposes the different discourses that compete for us. She shows, and this is very central to the book, the dilemma and crisis of the writer trying to make a fiction in the midst of a world in chaos, a world of newsprint and 'facts', as well as conventionalized views of relationships with all the hypocrisies and self-deceptions that can be found within them. As Gayle Greene comments (in *Changing the Story*, 1991: p. 116), 'Lessing says, everyone is "a prisoner of the assumptions and dogmas of his time, which he does not question, because he has never been told they exist" (p. xvi); as Anna says, "Well, surely the thought follows – what stereotype am I?" ' (*GN* 49). Doris Lessing is looking again at many of the problems she has already explored in earlier works, but here she sets them in new and exciting relationships with each other, in what Bakhtin terms dialogical relations with each other.

In one sense, Anna Wulf is portrayed as suffering from writer's block, while in another she is writing all the time in the notebooks which, as Gayle Greene says,

> contain commentary, explicit and implicit, on the ideological complicity of literary and critical forms – novels, short stories, journalism, parody, 'propaganda', literary criticism, reviews. Their discussion – and demonstration – of the complicity of forms with the systems, capitalist and communist, that produce them, offers a kind of 'worst possible case', exploring the possibility that all discourse is inextricably and inevitably bound to 'reproduction', bound to a circular process of reproducing the ideology which produces it, determined and determining. (Greene, 117)

Early in the Black Notebook, Anna records what she feels about the contemporary novel:

> The point is, that the function of the novel seems to be changing; it has become an outpost of journalism; we read novels for information about areas of life we don't know – Nigeria, South Africa, the American army, a coal-mining village, coteries in Chelsea, etc. We read to *find out what is going on* . . . I find that I read with the *same kind of curiosity* most novels, and a book of reportage. Most novels, if they are successful at all, are original in the sense that they report the existence of an area of society, a type of person, not yet admitted to the general literate consciousness . . . Human beings are so divided, are becoming more and more divided, *and more subdivided in themselves*, reflecting the world, that they reach out desperately, not knowing they do it, for information about other groups inside their own country, let alone about groups in other countries. It is a blind grasping out for their own wholeness . . . (*GN* 75)

And Anna admits her despair of ever writing 'the only kind of novel which interests me: a book powered with an intellectual or moral passion strong enough to create order, to create a new way of looking at life' (*GN* 76). Always Anna reminds us of what T. S. Eliot calls the 'intolerable wrestle | With words and meanings': 'She said to herself: I don't know why I still find it so hard to accept that words are faulty and by their very nature inaccurate. If I thought they were capable of expressing the truth I wouldn't keep journals which I refuse to let anyone see . . .' (*GN* 565). But despite all these statements, which not only illuminate Anna's state of mind but also shed light on Doris Lessing's novel; despite the ways in which *The Golden Notebook* explores areas of depersonalized union within relationships (where men and women not only interact but pool their abilities and insights) alongside fragmentations, anticipating thematically *The Four-Gated City*; despite the experiment with the novel as form, which the intricate divisions and continuities maintain by the splicing of notebooks and frame story; despite the dialogue between different ways of presenting fictions and the brilliant exposures of different readings of the same event, together with wilfully contrived mis-readings, the parodies built in, the pastiches; despite all these, Doris Lessing found, when she had finished the book, as she tells us in the later Preface, 'that I had written a tract about the sex war, and fast discovered that nothing I said then could change that diagnosis' (*GN* 10). Ironically, within *The Golden Notebook*, Anna had faced the trauma of having a book read very differently from her intention, in a brush with a television producer. Again, in a later dream (and dreams are always vital contributors to Doris Lessing's fiction), Anna is frightened by a jeering projectionist who runs films of her past, laughing at the credit 'Directed by Anna Wulf', and mocking her with: 'And what makes you think that the emphasis you have put on it is correct?' (*GN* 537).

In the preface to *The Golden Notebook* Doris Lessing comes to terms with the way her novel has been wrested from her. She sets her own reading of it against the way it has been read since its publication. She mentions three readings, which each concentrate exclusively on one aspect of the work (the sex war, politics, and mental illness) and observes that 'these incidents bring up again questions of what people see when they read a book, and why one person sees one pattern and nothing at all of another pattern, and how odd it is to have, as author, such a clear picture of a book, that is seen so very differently by its readers' (*GN* 20). Such diverse readings seem to me to reflect the dilemma Anna finds herself in at the beginning of *The Golden Notebook*, when she sees her notebooks as an attempt to impose order on formlessness and the chaos of the world she lives in. Doris Lessing's vision in her novel is in the end so all-embracing, speaks in such a huge diversity of languages, that many of her readers have tended to opt for partial engagement, for the voice they are most familiar with, the comfort of some one coherent strand rather than the impressive scope of the whole. And, at the end of her preface, Doris Lessing seems to accept this:

> ... it is not only childish of a writer to want readers to see what he sees, to understand the shape and aim of a novel as he sees it – his wanting this means that he has not understood a most fundamental point. Which is that the book is alive and potent and fructifying and able to promote thought and discussion *only* when its plan and shape and intention are not understood, because that moment of seeing the shape and plan and intention is also the moment when there isn't anything more to be got out of it. (*GN* 20–1)

Certainly *The Golden Notebook* became, almost as soon as it was published, a flagship for the reawakening women's movement, and it has continued to be claimed as a classic feminist text for, as Gayle Greene says, 'The central question of *The Golden Notebook* – how to oppose a system by means of linguistic and literary conventions that have been forged by that system – is a central question facing feminist theory today: can we use the master's tools to dismantle the master's house?' (Greene, 117; this last image refers to an article by Audre Lorde). Indeed, so clearly was Doris Lessing seen as a spokeswoman for women's rights (and her earlier novels could be read in this way) that any move away in subsequent books from issues considered central to feminist debate has been seen in some quarters as Doris Lessing betraying the cause – yet the issues raised in *The Golden Notebook* are ones she returns to again and again, exploring women's enslavement to conventions and/or their reshaping of their roles in such works as *The Summer before the Dark* (1973), *The Memoirs of a Survivor* (1974), and the 'Jane Somers' books (1983 and 1984).

But Doris Lessing refuses to be confined by one particular side of feminist debate: she sometimes explores the development of the individual as in *Martha Quest*, sometimes probes essentialism, the nature of woman rather than the individual, as in *The Marriages between Zones Three, Four and Five* (1980). It seems to me that, when exploring women's issues, Doris Lessing is concerned to set up dialogues between self and group, between essentialism and social bodies, and that these dialogues are spread over several works, meshing into networks of other issues. She seems to me to be questing for what Lois McNay describes in *Foucault and Feminism* (1992) when she says:

> In my view, a key task for feminists in the future is . . . to explore, for example, how outlining basic normative standards need not necessarily threaten the autonomy of the individual; how individual difference is better protected in a social environment based on tolerance and certain collective standards, rather than on a *laissez-faire* individualism; how a politics of self-actualization need not lapse inevitably into introversion but may contribute to wider forms of progressive social change. (p. 197)

And Doris Lessing is always primarily concerned with social change, with the social constraints on men and women as to their gender roles rather than with specific explorations of women in terms of solely sexual difference. In an article published in *Partisan Review* (1991) she speaks out against such feminisms as are biologically exclusive and those which pay too little homage to the achievements of feminists before 1968. In many ways her work supports Cora Kaplan's claim in 'Language and Gender' (in *Sea Changes: Essays on Culture and Feminism*) that 'There can in one sense be no feminist literary criticism, for any new theoretical approach to literature that uses gender difference as an important category involves a profoundly altered view of both sexes to language, speech, writing and culture' (p. 70). And this is precisely what we find in the culminating golden notebook of *The Golden Notebook*, where Anna writes the first sentence of Saul's new novel and he offers the first sentence of hers, each of them, as it were, inscribing the other's body. Anna thinks, 'I felt towards him as if he were my brother, as if, like a brother, it wouldn't matter how we strayed from each other, how far apart we were, we would always be flesh of one flesh, and think each other's thoughts' (*GN* 556).

What Anna Wulf is concerned for, and what she dreams of, is the role of what are termed 'the boulder-pushers' (*GN* 544), fighting to establish truths about a vast range of issues of which gender is only one. She says:

> There's a great black mountain. It's human stupidity. There are a group of people who push a boulder up the mountain. When they've got a few feet up, there's a war, or the wrong sort of revolution, and the boulder rolls down – not to the bottom, it always manages to end a few inches

higher than when it started. So the group of people put their shoulders to the boulder and start pushing again. (*GN* 544)

In the end, the boulder-pushers are Doris Lessing's prime concern, not only in *The Golden Notebook* but in all her work. And she never relies on one angle, one point of view. She says at the end of her preface to *The Golden Notebook*, 'And when a book's pattern and the shape of its inner life is as plain to the reader as it is to the author – then perhaps it is time to throw the book aside, as having had its day, and start again on something new' (*GN* 21).

This comment throws light on where Doris Lessing's own quest as a writer is taking her, and indeed she confirms that writing *The Golden Notebook* changed her: 'When I had finished it I knew I had either to pretend I had not had new ideas, intimations, experiences . . . or accept that I could no longer be the same person. To be precise: I could no longer accept the contemporary "package" ' (*DLR* 460). Having explored Communism and learnt from it (as she says in the original endnote to *Going Home*) 'the realities of political power', she moves on to explore how the non-rational (as defined by Western society) may expand humankind's perception of itself. This search leads to an area explored by Michel Foucault in his *Madness and Civilization* (1961) and by R. D. Laing in such works as *The Divided Self* (1965) and *The Politics of Experience* (1967). Foucault looks at how, up to the Renaissance,

the sensibility to madness was linked to the presence of imaginary transcendences. In the classical age [i.e. late seventeenth-century France], for the first time, madness was perceived through a condemnation of idleness and . . . a moral perception sustains and animates [this view] . . . Hence the Hôpital does not have the appearance of a mere refuge for those whom age, infirmity, or sickness keep from working; it will have not only the aspect of a forced labour camp, but also that of a moral institution responsible for punishing, for correcting a certain moral 'abeyance' which does not merit the tribunal of men, but cannot be corrected by the severity of penance alone. (Foucault, 136-7)

Laing, whose work interested Doris Lessing in the 1960s, explores the implications of such ideas for contemporary society, and the way in which power structures within society can cause the individual to become an outsider, alienated. In *The Divided Self* (1965) he shows what are termed sanity and madness as degrees of conjunction and disjunction between two persons where the one is sane by common

22

consent; in *The Politics of Experience* (1967) he asserts: 'Madness need not be all breakdown. It may also be break-through. It is potentially liberation and renewal as well as enslavement and existential death' (p. 110).

This attitude to madness, to breakdown, is explored in *The Golden Notebook*, and plays a very important part in the last two 'Martha Quest' books and *Briefing for a Descent into Hell* (1971). Doris Lessing's affinity with Laing is clear as she returns to Children of Violence, with *Landlocked* (1965). While this novel concludes the volumes dealing with Martha's life in Southern Rhodesia, new elements, a new perspective, are evident. The epigraph suggests one way in which the text can be read as it records a teaching story, questioning easy assumptions about identity. The novel, while pursuing Martha's life, challenges such assumptions; public life breaks down after the war, the white-black relationship wavers, and people like Mrs Van who had been leaders of social change are bypassed; Anton, the precisely orthodox Communist, is shown as capable of capitalistic posturing to safeguard his position; and Martha's lover, Thomas Stern, breaks down, and, as he disintegrates before what appears to be a vast spiritual revelation (his notes on this will be taken up in *The Four-Gated City*), he even changes radically in physical appearance. And Martha realizes that she hardly knows herself.

All these themes were germinating in *The Golden Notebook* and will be explored again in the novels of the 1970s. As I have already suggested, one of the fascinating things about Doris Lessing's writing is the way in which her works interrelate and interrogate one another. It is in one sense ludicrous to talk about development in any linear sense (although development in another sense is obvious), since the same ground is probed and reprobed, never repetitively, but to focus on some perspective in one book which was merely glimpsed in another. So, in *Landlocked*, the love that Martha shares with Thomas Stern, where their total oneness helps each to learn or at least acknowledge something very profoundly personal about themselves as individuals, echoes the culminating relationships of Anna and Saul, Anna and Milt, in *The Golden Notebook*. This then is a marked feature of Doris Lessing's work: it is both utterly engaged with the world contemporary with the time of writing and continually reviewing past material in different guises and always with fresh insights. So, in *Landlocked*, Martha's mother's mind is explored with great sensitivity, as Mr Quest dies and she looks back at a life of disappointed expectations; there are echoes of *The Grass is Singing* in this, but also anticipations of *The Memoirs of a Survivor*, as here, in Mrs Quest's repeated dream of roses given to her by her mother:

> Mrs Quest drifted towards sleep. The scent of roses came in through the window, and she smiled. This time they remained in her hand – three crimson roses. The brutal woman, her beautiful mother, remained invisible in her dangerous heaven. The painful girl, Martha, was locked in her bedroom, under orders from Court and Judge. Mrs Quest had become her own comforter, her own solace. Having given birth to herself, she cradled Mrs Quest, a small, frightened girl, who lay in tender arms against a breast covered in the comfort of bright salmon-pink, home-knitted wool. (*L.* 98)

Landlocked may well appear as a transitional work between *The Golden Notebook* and later work, but its explorations of true selves and false selves set up in response to society's tyrannical discourses are compassionately and perceptively achieved. And the book's ironies do not have the bitterness of those in *A Ripple from the Storm*.

The last volume of Children of Violence, *The Four-Gated City*, was published in 1969. It is a novel which complements *The Golden Notebook* in the way it organizes a vast range of post-war experiences into a form which, like the earlier work, proclaims the unity within diversity, and which captures a great deal of the vitality, confusions, and contradictions of the Sixties. As Ruth Whittaker argues, in her book *Doris Lessing*, 'the narrative movement is not so much linear as concentric, with Martha at the centre of three overlapping worlds: the outside world of politics and wars, the immediate community of the Coldridge family, and the inner world of her expanding consciousness. Doris Lessing shows how these three circles affect one another . . .' (p. 54). Political developments of the post-war years are skilfully portrayed within the Coldridge family, for instance, with a grandmother who is a political hostess, an uncle who has defected to the Soviet Union, a father who nears breaking-point as he strives to hang on to his socialist ideals in a world of Cold War and witch-hunts, and a younger generation who set up a commune in the country. This complex Sixties context of Martha's continuing quest for wholeness is demonstrably also the main shaping force for the form that quest takes; and although Doris Lessing, in her Author's Notes, says 'This book is what the Germans call a *Bildungsroman*' (FGC 667), she offers a label which teases, much as the epigraph (a dervish teaching story) teases the reader. For, while the novel does indeed follow Martha's life in linear sequence, from her arrival in England to her death, she undergoes a sea-change as she progresses. The voices of the first pages place Martha in a realistic post-war Britain among the kind of working-class characters first found in Doris Lessing's non-fictional work, *In Pursuit of the English*, published in 1960, which describes the household she entered when she herself first came to England. But very soon the perspective of *The Four-Gated City* shifts, as Martha enters the house of the Coldridges; she slowly but surely moves from the focus of attention and becomes instead a participator in a group development, observing and learning alongside a complex set of characters as they battle to come to terms with themselves and their role in an increasingly violent and disintegrating world. We see Mark learning, for example, as he (echoing Anna Wulf in *The Golden Notebook*) papers his study with factual articles from newspapers and journals about happenings in the world outside, while trying to make sense of Thomas Stern's incoherent account of his vision for a future society. Meanwhile Martha wrestles with various aspects of her own identity, trying to understand, for example, the way she dons false personalities to cope with the contemporary world (and such false selves are discussed by Laing in his studies of how people cope with alienation): in certain contexts she becomes what she calls 'The Defender', who 'got shrill, exclamatory, didactic, hectoring, and went off at a word into long speeches' (*FGC* 143); while in other contexts she becomes what she calls 'Matty' (as this is a role she has assumed from adolescence), 'the clumsy self-denigrating clown' (*FGC* 143). And Martha tries to shed these false personalities. Through people struggling to know themselves, Doris Lessing explores how they become more in tune with other people, their alienation left behind together with the society which generated it. Towards the end of the book, people even assume each other's identities for a time, an idea which will be explored years later in *The Making of the Representative for Planet 8*, published in 1982.

The Four-Gated City already shows Doris Lessing's appreciation of the advantages and perils of using space fiction as a means of exploring social and cultural issues and the inner space of the mind. Not only are the lives of Martha and her partners extended in practice into a post-holocaust future, but the potential of space fiction as a medium is explored throughout the book. For example, Jimmy,

Mark's scientist partner at the factory, writes space fiction. Martha tries to find out where he gets his plots, as he has just written two very successful novels about 'people who had more senses than are considered normal' (FGC 392). He says the ideas are just ' "in the air" . . . and went on to say that "all of us" wrote about such ideas. He meant, by "all of us" other space fiction writers. He then went on to describe a new machine which he was working on that could stimulate or destroy areas of the brain . . .' (FGC 392). Jimmy, terrifyingly, has insight but no sense of moral responsibility for his ideas. Mark, on the other hand, uses all his faculties to attempt to secure humanity's future. His visionary novel of a future society is at first rejected by publishers who 'said with commendable frankness that they would not publish a communist' (FGC 314). But eventually the book is 'taken up by the science fiction addicts . . . of course such work was not then taken seriously in literary circles, but he found their way of looking at the world nearer to his own than any other' (FGC 314–5). The despised science-fiction writers are shown with Swiftian irony to be more in tune with ideas for the future salvation of humankind that the publishers who label Mark a Communist and therefore unacceptable. Yet Doris Lessing does not go overboard in their favour: Jimmy's failure of responsibility is as evident as Mark's moral integrity.

The web of voices in The Four-Gated City is tightly woven, with languages of politics, science, psychology, literary criticism, sex and gender issues, past, present, and future, all interacting. Contemporary languages within society are ironized and parodied, and the capacity to share and explore inner space, first encountered in The Golden Notebook, is used here to investigate potential changes in the way society might operate to ensure a human future. Futuristic fable enables the final pages of The Four-Gated City to look beyond the present painful experiments with breakdown, which Martha and Linda attempt, to what might happen if the mind expansion they strive for should become a reality. The seeds for Doris Lessing's space-fiction series, the five Canopus in Argos books, are here. But other works precede them, the next novel being published in 1971.

4

Explorations of
Inner Space

Briefing for a Descent into Hell picks upon the potential inherent in
space fiction suggested in *The Four-Gated City*, as it acknowledges in
its subtitle, which reads: '*Category*: Inner-space fiction|For there is
never anywhere to go but in'. This is the story of a man found
'wandering on the Embankment near Waterloo Bridge' (*BDH* 11),
apparently rambling in speech and suffering from loss of memory.
He is taken to hospital and placed under the care of doctors X and
Y, who cannot agree as to the treatment he should be given.
Eventually he is given electric shock treatment and restored to
'normality', the life of a married Professor of Classics who, when
'cured', repudiates all the experiences (and he has revealed a rich
inner life) which he has had while 'ill'.

But such a précis of the plot is utterly misleading, for Doris Lessing
leaves linear narrative behind, interspersing doctors' reports, dis-
cussions, questioning of and reaction to the patient, and the piecing
together of his 'normal' life, with vivid accounts of his journey
through inner space on a mission of crucial importance for humanity,
a mission made ever more difficult because earth's atmosphere (and
it is earth, not breakdown, which is the hell of the title) makes it hard
to remember the purpose of the quest. The novel is therefore based
on irony: the doctors, whose names are denied to us throughout, are
trying to restore the patient to 'normality', to his 'name' and
'memory', but in doing so they unwittingly destroy his inner-space
normality, identity, and chance to retrieve the memory of his mission.

What *Briefing* gives us is a series of Bakhtinian voices, languages,
which cannot talk to one another. This is made clear in a section on
the 'gods' which contains both parodies of conference discourse and
meditations on the linking and merging of individuals; there is much
here (especially in the conference mode) that is being satirized, but
we cannot assume, given the argument of the novel, that, if words

are mocked, then the ideas which the words have to express are mocked as well. These 'gods' are responsible for sending the protagonist on his mission, and we hear Merc (a wittily modern Mercury), among others, warning him of the properties of Hell (earth) and of how

> each individual of this species [humankind] is locked up inside his own skull, his own personal experience – or believes that he is – and while a great part of their ethical systems, religious systems, etc., state the Unity of Life, even the most recent religion, which, being the most recent, is the most powerful, called Science, has only very fitful and inadequate gleams of insight into the fact that life is One. In fact, the distinguishing feature of this new religion, and why it has proved so inadequate, is its insistence on dividing off, compartmenting, pigeon-holing, and one of the most lamentable of these symptoms is its suspicion of and clumsiness with words. (*BDH* 120–1)

We find this diagnosis confirmed in *Briefing*, as the doctors do not consider what the protagonist's words may convey, what is actually going on in his head, as important, except as manifestations of his illness. They are presented as literal-minded, searching for clues to his 'real' identity (defined according to society's formulations). They never take seriously the poetry of his sea voyage, where

> The sea is saltier here than close inshore. A salt, salt sea, the brine coming flecked off the horses' jaws to mine. On my face, thick crusts of salt. I can taste it. Tears, seawater. I can taste salt from the sea. From the desert. The deserted sea. Sea horses. Dunes. The wind flicks sand from the crest of the dunes, spins off the curl of waves. (*BDH* 12)

Here the language proclaims the links within experience, not otherness; the 'play' with words affirms unity.

As the protagonist pours out the stories of his inner life, we are given a rich reworking of the Fall, of the origin of a discourse of savagery and oppression, of misogyny and racial antagonisms. But each time the protagonist is near recapturing his purpose, the doctors change his treatment, driving him into a different kind of adventure within inner space. And here again the ironies are rich and complex. For at one point the 'real' Charles (the Charles of the hospital ward) looks as if he is getting his memory back, recalling vividly a wartime mission in Yugoslavia. The language here is of the so-called realistic novel, but we are being teased on more than one level. Eventually we learn, or think we learn, that these experiences are not the protagonist's but those of a friend; so they are fictions of someone else's fact, and realism is a misleading mode devised to deceive us. Or is it? Remembering previous episodes in *The Golden Notebook*, *Landlocked*, and *The Four-Gated City*, where characters have for a while assumed one another's identities, is the protagonist's mind here merely demonstrating that he is *not* just 'locked up inside his own skull, his own personal experience' (*BDH* 120)? While the Fall episode shows him as tapping into folk memory, here he has tapped into a friend's memory. The doctors do not see the implications of this experience except as a threat to his 'normality', but we as readers are certainly urged, in the latter part of the book, to explore words carefully as inadequate tools by the recurring quotation from T. S. Eliot's 'Sweeney Agonistes': 'I gotta use words when I talk to you.' If this is Doris Lessing inviting us to deconstruct her own texts, it is surely a very specific kind of deconstruction that this text invites: to probe words for clues as much as for treachery; to probe for meanings that the words fail to express; not surely to resort to the nihilism of thinking that, if words do not convey meaning, meaning therefore vanishes.

A further irony is reserved for the endnote, where Doris Lessing tells of once writing a story for a film based on 'a close friendship with a man whose senses were different from the normal person's' (*BDH* 251). She wanted to show, she says, how such enhanced perception 'must be a handicap in a society organized as ours is, to favour the conforming, the average, the obedient' (*BDH* 251). But (and Doris Lessing's experience recalls Foucault's insights and R. D. Laing's clinical findings), film-makers could only ask: 'What is wrong with the man in the film?' (*BDH* 251). This experience led her to observe that 'one has to be particularly trained to believe that to put a label on a feeling, a state of mind . . . to find a set of words or a phrase; in short, to describe it; is the same as understanding and experiencing it' (*BDH* 251). Perhaps to test the truth of this observation, she decided to send her script to two medical specialists, for a diagnosis of what was wrong with the man. 'But their skilled and compassionate diagnoses, while authoritative, were quite different from each other's. They agreed about nothing at all' (*BDH* 252).

I have paused over this endnote, because *Briefing* was published after the preface was added to *The Golden Notebook*, in which Doris Lessing writes of the experience of losing control of the 'meaning' of her book. The endnote to *Briefing* can be read, therefore, as a hint at her own reading of this text, and picks up once more on the problem, and maybe the futility, of attempting to fix identity according to the formulae of society.

In 1973, two years after *Briefing for a Descent into Hell* came out, *The Summer before the Dark* was published. Here Doris Lessing again introduces someone who lives for a time in a world other than her usual one, but no longer within the context of space fiction. The protagonist is a woman in her forties, the novel a return to realism, and the focus on a summer when the woman takes a job away from her family and lives, not as the mother whose function and identity are defined by her service to and for the family, but as a career woman and then, as this role ends and her summer lover becomes ill, as a woman *per se* who learns to construct her own female identity through breakdown and the friends who take her in. The ending of the novel could be taken as ambivalent; the woman returns to her family with her new sense of herself intact, but the title of the book could suggest that its protagonist might well, if she were to survive the book's closure, suffer the same fate as the protagonist of *Briefing*, and forget her sense of her own wholeness once her earlier role and the identity which that had imposed upon her reasserted themselves.

But then again, perhaps not. Throughout her reinventing of herself, Kate has had a recurring dream of a seal stranded inland which she must return to the sea and, just before she returns to the family, she dreams that she does indeed release it: 'She saw that the sun was in front of her, not behind, not far far behind, under the curve of the earth, which was where it had been for so long. She looked at it, a large, light, brilliant, buoyant, tumultuous sun that seemed to sing' (*SD* 230). In *Asia* Doris Lessing speaks of the importance of full engagement with ordinary life, not retreat from society and its demands. So perhaps one can read the text as offering hope that Kate will hold on to her new sense of herself.

The following year, 1974, *The Memoirs of a Survivor* was published. Doris Lessing has referred to this novel as a kind of autobiography, but it is not in realistic mode. Just as *The Four-Gated City* reinvented the concept of the *Bildungsroman* by reaching into a future of evolving humankind, so *Memoirs* reinvents autobiography, interleaving an apocalyptic representation of the outer world with glimpses of the protagonist's inner life. The main action takes place within this protagonist's flat (the protagonist being a middle-aged woman without a stated name), from which she observes the world outside. And it is indeed an apocalyptic world; the 'children of violence' who supplied the title for the Martha Quest sequence now literally walk the streets; gangs of children move together, uprooted, plundering and scavenging amidst the wreckage of a disintegrating city. Yet, at the same time, what is shown, while often graphically frightening, is a form of social evolution instigated by the anarchic children; and one reading could be that this is not a futuristic fable but a fabular account of the late 1960s and early 1970s.

This is clearly a possible reading in the light of the behaviour of the young girl, Emily, who has been brought to the protagonist – for her protection? her education? that of the girl or the woman? None of this is clearly defined, for the very good reason that the observer and the observed are organically linked by what goes on in the world of inner space which occupies large sections of the novel. And the narrator, who appears to be observer rather than participant, watches Emily's growth, first resisting and then accepting, as the girl matches her maturing to the evolution of the other young people, as here:

> Chrysalis after chrysalis was outgrown, and then . . . [Emily] asked abruptly and gracelessly but in her over-polite and *awful* way for some more money, and went off by herself to the markets. She came back with some secondhand clothes that in one giant's step took her from being a child with fantastic visions of herself into a girl – a woman, rather . . . Now I thought that probably the heroes of the pavement would be beneath her; that she, a young woman, would demand what nature would in fact have chosen for her, a young man of seventeen, eighteen, even more.
>
> But the crowd, the pack, the gang – not yet a tribe, but on its way to being one – had suffered forced growth, as she had. A few weeks had done it. (*MS* 56)

And is the narrator merely observing? In the flat, perhaps, but certainly this is not true of the inner life which she enters through the homely wall of her flat (recalling the wall Linda banged her head against in *The Four-Gated City*, when she was trying to escape the confines of social constraint through mind expansion). In inner space she endeavours to repair the damage to the family home, and in the process meets images of family cycles, trapping each generation, just as Martha perceived Mrs Quest and herself being trapped in *A Proper Marriage*, where, as I quoted earlier, 'she saw her mother, a prim-faced Edwardian schoolgirl, confronting . . . the Victorian father, the patriarchal father, with rebellion. She saw herself sitting where her mother now sat . . . opposite her, a young woman of whom she could distinguish nothing clearly but a set, obstinate face . . .'

(*PM* 126). Recalling this passage, it is easy to read *Memoirs* as autobiography, as we watch the protagonist's efforts to 'set the house in order' so that, by the end of the novel, she can redeem herself, her predecessors, and the society of children, leading them through the wall. This is a vision of what might have been, if the protagonist of *Briefing* had been able to fulfil his mission and wake society out of its zombie existence. It shows in fable form, I would suggest, the result of self-knowledge, and the 'woman' the protagonist finally glimpses, 'the one person I had been looking for all this time', though not described here, surely recalls a passage in *Landlocked*, where

> Martha knew that, if she could not trust her judgement, or rather, if her judgement of outside things, people, was like a light that grew brighter, harsher, as the area it covered grew smaller, she could trust with her life . . . the monitor, the guardian, who stood somewhere, *was* somewhere in this shell of substance, smooth brown flesh so pleasantly curved into the shape of young woman with smooth browny-gold hair, alert dark eyes. (*L.* 23)

But for *Memoirs* there is no preface, no endnote, no epigraph. The fable stands vividly and teasingly on its own, with nothing explained, including Emily's pet Hugo, a mixture of cat and dog. This novel is primarily a fictionalizing of historical fact, both public and private, an experiment in reconciling a language of violent social change with one of striving towards self-knowledge. The final images of the concluding paragraphs poignantly evoke the poetry and optimism of the dawning of the Age of Aquarius at the beginning of the 1970s:

> Beside her, then, as she turned to walk on and away and ahead while the world folded itself up around her, was Emily, and beside Emily was Hugo, and lingering after them Gerald. Emily, yes, but quite beyond herself, transmuted, and in another key, and the yellow beast Hugo fitted her new self: a splendid animal, handsome, all kindly dignity and command, he walked beside her and her hand was on his neck. Both walked quickly behind that One who went ahead showing them the way out of this collapsed little world into another order of world altogether. Both, just for an instant, turned their faces as they passed that other threshold. They smiled . . . seeing those faces, Gerald was drawn after them, but still he hesitated in a fearful conflict, looking back and around, while the brilliant fragments whirled around him. And then, at the very last moment, they came, his children came running, clinging to his hands and his clothes, and they all followed quickly on after the others as the last walls dissolved. (*MS* 190)

5

Canopus in Argos: Archives

Briefing and *Memoirs* act, in retrospect, as forerunners of Doris Lessing's next five novels, the series called Canopus in Argos: Archives. The five novels form a series rather than a sequence, because, although some of the characters do turn up in the different books, there is no continuity from one work to the next. Throughout, Doris Lessing makes use of discourses of space fiction to defamiliarize human history and certain areas of human cultures and experience. This is no departure into escapist fantasy: there are all the established concerns for social, political, and spiritual ideas; for individuals either rejected or absorbed by the group; for experiment with form; and for the continuing awareness of the treachery of words, particularly when they are most taken for granted. But there are also new elements.

In each of the novels, Doris Lessing shifts her focus so that the reader, as in *Briefing* and *Memoirs*, is persuaded into working for interpretations. Some equations (as, for instance, in the racial tensions between north and south on Shikasta, or the increasingly problematized relationship between the Canopus Empire and its colonials) may appear irresistibly obvious, others less so; and, judging by the variety of response to the various works, what may seem obvious to one reader is far from obvious to another (some literal-minded critics assuming that the mere use of the word 'Empire' must condone imperialism), while the very fact that Doris Lessing writes space fiction at all has dismayed a number of critics.

In her preface to the first novel, *Re: Colonised Planet 5, Shikasta* (1979), Doris Lessing says:

> The old 'realistic' novel is being changed . . . because of influences from
> that genre loosely described as space fiction. Some people regret this. I
> was in the States, giving a talk, and the professor who was acting as

chairwoman, and whose only fault was that perhaps she had fed too long on the pieties of academia, interrupted me with: 'If I had you in my class you'd never get away with that!' . . . I had been saying that space fiction, with science fiction, makes up the most original branch of literature now; it is inventive and witty; it has already enlivened all kinds of writing; and that literary academics and pundits are much to blame for patronizing or ignoring it. (CP 9)

This first book of the series, *Shikasta*, is packed with ideas. It offers an awesomely impressive view of human history, which is shown as if through a high-speed camera, catching the peculiar behavioural patterns of an aggressive and endangered species, and very disconcerting it is. The different languages (of the bureaucratic imperialists who observe us, of the ideologies that govern our actions, of the individuals caught up in the network of voices competing for their attention in a neocontemporary/near future time full of confusions and contradictions), these different languages are presented under headings (as in official documentary reports) with different typefaces. The sheer range of ideas confronted in this novel and crowding the pages, all of them relevant to the world we live in, have been found by some readers to be too densely packed for comfortable reading. The lay-out of the novel may offer the security of compartmentalizing, but the overall effect of the work is a challenge to confront the chaos of the contemporary world, its savagely competitive discourses of power, its all-too-frequent failure to achieve the kind of dialogues which would render compartmentalizing redundant.

Yet, amidst all the anarchy, squalor, and dangerous power struggles, hope is offered, as it was in *Memoirs*, as it was in *The Four-Gated City*: a hope of a form of evolution which will leave behind what a future speaker sees as (sees present humankind as) 'our ancestors, the poor animal-men, always murdering and destroying because they couldn't help it' (CP 447). No, this is not a comfortable book, but it dares to be optimistic while facing, clear-eyed, the world we inhabit. It is Doris Lessing's peculiar brand of courage that she can both confront what is going on world-wide with appalling clarity and resort to neither escapism nor nihilism as a way out.

In all five of these works, she has chosen to write the kind of space fiction that takes an extraterrestrial (though not always superhuman) standpoint rather than an earthly one, so as to help the process of defamiliarization. But she also presents us, in these five books, with a number of extraterrestrial observers with very different points of view, so that readers are discouraged from assuming that they are confronting the author herself. For instance, the main character in the first book (*Shikasta*) is Johor of Canopus. The impression he gives in this first book is perfectly familiar to readers of space fiction: he is a representative of a super-race, dedicated, at considerable risk to himself, to helping a poorly evolved species which shares most of our contemporary problems. He reappears in the fourth book (*The Making of the Representative for Planet 8* (1982)) in much the same role, although more as a sharer than an official, with very different lessons to teach and very different teaching techniques. But in the third and fifth books the main representative of Canopus is Klorathy, who is markedly different from Johor: he is far more susceptible to contamination by what he has come to confront, so providing us with an unreliable narrator and with an ironic representation of the follies of Empire and its servants. This is explicitly shown in the third book (*The Sirian Experiments* (1981), where, incidentally, some readers have pounced on the female protagonist as their Lessing surrogate), and wittily hinted at in the fifth book (*Documents Relating to the Sentimental Agents in the Volyen Empire* (1983)).

The second book (*The Marriages between Zones Three, Four and Five* (1980)) is one of the two novels of the series (the other being *The Making of the Representative for Planet 8*) narrated by a colonial rather than a representative of the ruling power. On one level, this is a delicately erotic love-story. On another, it offers a lyrical fable of two aspects of the 'female', one with a refining sensitivity threatened by its own refinement with sterility, the other a splendid animal and initially nothing more. Their two realms flank the 'male' domain of heroics and war. The setting is strongly reminiscent of Persian miniature paintings, of Middle Eastern tales set in medieval times. The central characters speak to each other at first in languages which are mutually incomprehensible, and part of their task is to invent a new language which they can share. The fable is developed through the ironies of mutual misunderstanding on all levels into a celebration of emotion and passion and, through these, into a celebration of the need for light and dark, 'daylight selves' and the energy of their 'shadow side', if genuine evolution and growth are to be achieved. As in *Shikasta*, Doris Lessing portrays evolution as painful. The narrator, the Chronicler of the story, for example, asserts

the need to fear what is evil, since 'Describing, we become' and 'even
. . . summon'. But he acknowledges, none the less, that

> there is a mystery here and it is not one that I understand: without this
> sting of otherness, of – even – the vicious, without the terrible energies
> of the underside of health, sanity, sense, then nothing works or *can* work.
> I tell you that goodness – what we in our ordinary daylight selves call
> goodness: the ordinary, the decent – these are nothing without the hidden
> powers that pour forth continually from their shadow sides. Their hidden
> aspects contained and tempered. (*MZ* 243)

This hesitant attempt at understanding the opposites on which
personal and social stability and development rest lies at the heart
of *Marriages*, but in stressing this I have not begun to convey the
lyrical beauty of the tale, which is one of Doris Lessing's most
triumphant celebrations of love while at the same time containing,
easily and without being pompous, the insights of the Chronicler.
And the choices facing artists when trying to convey matters of
importance to an audience with definite cultural expectations as to
what ought to be happening is also explored, throwing light, I cannot
help feeling, on the problem facing any novelist wanting to engage
with matters of historical importance to her society. There are
moments, for instance, when artists who want to present their
subjects in the most attractive light invent in their fictions something
which appears to distort historical fact, as the Chronicler frequently
acknowledges, describing first romantic representations and then
what really happened, as here:

> This scene is always depicted thus: there is a star-crowded sky, a slice of
> bright moon, and the soldier striding forward made visible and prominent
> because his chest armour and headpiece and his shield are shining. Beside
> him Al-Ith is visible only as a dark shadow, but her eyes gleam softly
> out from her veil.
> It could not have been anything like this. The wind was straight in their
> faces, strong and cold. She wrapped her head completely in her veil, and
> he had his cloak tight about him and over the lower part of his face; and
> the shield was held to protect them both from the wind. (*MZ* 25)

And yet even such a romantic distortion of fact actually conveys a
truth which the facts fail to acknowledge: Al-Ith *is* in shadow while
the soldier's role is assertive and oppressive, since he is taking her
to her arranged and (at this stage in the story) unwelcome marriage
with his king; and the soldier's ostentatious armour *is* an important

issue, since Al-Ith's role is to soften the machismo of his zone. *Marriages* weaves story, the art of story-telling, and the implications of the choice of subject-matter into an utterly delightful whole.

In *Marriages* we are also told how story-tellers, Chroniclers, indeed 'any of us', are all linked and, because aspects of a whole, are constantly shifting identities, which explains why story-tellers fictionalize whatever fact is, since the 'truth' is both crucial and hard to convey:

> We are the visible and evident aspects of a whole we all share, that we all go to form. Al-Ith was, for most of her life, queen . . . the substance of Zone Three expressed itself in her in that shape . . . queen. Or at other times mother, friend, animal-knower. And when she went down to Zone Four how may we assess the way Zone Three squeezed and forced itself in there, as Ben Ata's wife, queen of that place with him, Yori's protector, Dabeeb's friend . . . yes, but what are all these guises, aspects, presentations? Only manifestations of *what we all are* at different times, according to how these needs are pulled out of us. I write in these bald words the deepest lessons of my life, the truest substance of what I have learned. (MZ 242)

I have quoted these passages from *Marriages*, since they not only illuminate that fable, but also clarify a guiding principle which manifests itself in all Doris Lessing's work. It is part of her power as a writer that she openly offers us such comments, not only as an apologia for representation in art but as an explanation of how society works in real life.

Marriages acknowledges the importance of extremes in maintaining a proper balance within the individual and society. But there can be other kinds of extreme, extremes generated by the environment in which inner lives operate, which can paradoxically encourage growth, understanding. In *The Making of the Representative for Planet 8*, a community of men and women (whose culture involves changing and exchanging their social roles as need arises, just as Al-Ith's Chronicler describes) are faced with the extinction of their planet. In their distress, they are joined by Johor, who remains with them to the last, helping them to learn a new language to cope with their loss. Although some critics have seen this novel's central theme as mystical, it can also be read as a fable questioning ideas of identity (following on from the questions raised in *Marriages*). For instance, characters are called by the names of their trades (Doeg –

memory-maker and keeper of records; Masson – the builder; Pedug – representative for education). However, as the crisis approaches, the Canopean Johor helps each, by a method similar to Socratic questioning, to see that, since they have in the past changed trades, they have also changed identities, their trades forming part of those identities. And, once the characters can accept such changes, they are ready for an evolutionary change, melding and merging as the end comes, for 'we understood that everything in us was new, being new-made, new-worked, changed . . . we were being changed, molecule by molecule, atom by atom . . . Thoughts . . . that once we had regarded tolerantly, or with approval, as necessary, were now being rejected by what we had become' (*MRP* 136). This novel's fabular qualities become clearer when we remember Doris Lessing's insistence in the late preface to *The Golden Notebook* that 'we must not divide things off, must not compartmentalize' (*GN* 10). Remembering that comment in the preface is also important when looking at the libretto (based on *Representative*) which she wrote for an opera composed by Philip Glass in 1988, and performed by the English National Opera in the 1988/9 season. In the published libretto, the emphasis is markedly on not compartmentalizing, and this is picked up in the music.

As I have suggested, this fable can be read literally or on a number of levels; it can be read as a story of selfless courage and comradeship in the face of disaster; it can be read as a parable of social change; it can be read as a reconciliation of destruction and creation. In all the space-fiction series, Doris Lessing shows how, over the years, she has learnt that the audience, the reader, is not necessarily going to see things the way the writer intends them, and so she gives us fable to play with. And, on whatever level one reads her work, she is superb at dealing with what can be quaintly termed grey areas – certainly, for example, in *Documents Relating to the Sentimental Agents in the Volyen Empire*, the final volume of the 'Archives'.

This novel teases its readers with its subtle probing of the grey area between reason and the non-rational. Its target for satire is the abuse of words on a planet troubled by an infectiously diseased rhetoric, and yet (as it demonstrates most wittily) words must be used to express the abuse. We are invited to see characters who are as vulnerable to the effects of, say, emotive rhetoric when they are least aware of it, as when they accept their plight. On several occasions Klorathy shows himself aware that he (like his more vulnerable pupil, Incent) is succumbing to the disease of 'false' rhetoric (cliché, jargon, and so on); but the reader has to be doubly vigilant when Klorathy does not express such a fear. At the very beginning of the book, for example, Klorathy reports that his pupil Incent 'did succumb to an attack of Rhetoric' (*SA* 11), and 'Rhetoric' is clearly a term used pejoratively by logical Canopus. Klorathy must refer to emotive rhetoric, yet the preamble to his report on Incent is charged with emotion:

> I requested leave from service on Shikasta; I find myself on a planet whose dominant feature is the same as Shikasta's. Very well! I will stick it out for this term of duty. But I hereby give notice, *formally*, that I am applying to be sent, when I'm finished here, to a planet as backward as you like, as challenging as you like, but not one whose populations seem permanently afflicted by self-destructive dementia. (*SA* 11)

We are then given Incent's own report as proof of the younger agent's succumbing to 'Rhetoric', but the honesty of this report, coming after Klorathy's initial outburst, is striking:

> This was the terrible Shammat! This wonderful being who wept as the rebels were led out to execution! . . . I was quite ashamed to see Krolgul's ironic but kind smile when I spoke of the Volyen Empire with what I am afraid I now see as something not far from contempt . . .
> . . . I realized, and with what shock and distress I hardly dare to say, that my attitude was no longer consistent with that of a loyal servant of Canopus.
> I am prepared to offer my resignation. What shall I do? (*SA* 12)

Certainly Incent's language refers more openly to emotional reactions than Klorathy's; but Incent also offers a diagnosis of his own problem – demonstrating in the process, incidentally, that he has been swayed as much by behaviour as by words – whereas Klorathy seems unaware of his own incipient hysteria (despite his humiliating experiences recorded in *The Sirian Experiments*). The problem for readers is made more teasing by Klorathy's response to Incent's report:

> I did not reply to this, though, of course, had he resigned I would have asked him to reconsider. But he did not . . .
> Volyen itself seethes with emotions of all kinds . . . to the extent that there is nowhere I could place Incent hoping he would be free from the stimulus of words long enough to recover his balance . . . as you know,

I am always unwilling to waste such experiences in young officials who might be strengthened by them in the long run. (*SA* 12–13)

These three extracts demonstrate the challenge that readers face from the very beginning of *Sentimental Agents*. We are given, in quick succession, Klorathy's near hysterical rejection of 'Rhetoric'; Incent's emotional but perceptive analysis of his own succumbing to Shammat's expressions of emotion; and Klorathy's apparently rational decision about Incent. But has Klorathy's rational reaction been undercut by his initial outburst on his own behalf? Or does that initial outburst offer a more mature demonstration of how to cope with emotional stress than Incent's open use of emotive vocabulary and graphic analysis of his own predicament? Certainly Klorathy does not ask, as Incent does, 'What shall I do?' Doris Lessing leaves her readers to make up their own minds; she leaves a great deal to her readers' response to language and its relation to meaning throughout the novel.

And readers' responses have been mixed. The parodies of bureaucratic, journalistic, and legal styles, the exposures of emotional rhetoric alongside the more subtly devious questioning of logic, have led some critics to maintain that, in this final work of the series, the narrative succeeds in deconstructing Canopus itself. Certainly the Canopus narrators are vulnerable to rhetorical diseases; but, since all the characters in the novel are equally vulnerable, it follows that all their empires, including Canopus, must be seen to be at risk. A phrase running through the book ('Empires rise and fall, rise and fall') is used both by the narrators and by a wide variety of the characters they describe. But, as in *Briefing*, it would be rash to assume that the finite natures of these 'Empires' imply nihilism. It is worth recalling that the extinction of Planet 8 in *The Making of the Representative* actually initiates the 'making' of its representative, and that Johor of Canopus shares both the death throes and the rebirth of the planet's population. So *Sentimental Agents* can be read as offering a dynamic reappraisal of the slogan 'Empires rise and fall', since one of the most fascinating challenges offered to readers by its narrative voices is the marked closeness of Canopus and its archenemy Shammat. Their differences, indeed, may complement one another, may (recalling the passage quoted earlier from *Marriages*) need the 'sting of otherness' to work. At one point Klorathy asks Johor whether Canopus is not too bound to logic, while elsewhere he describes how he is moved by certain Shammat-inspired emotions. Are these reactions weakness or strength? Doris Lessing leaves it to her readers to decide.

The link between Canopus and Shammat is startlingly emphasized towards the end of the narrative in a conversation that Klorathy reports between himself and Krolgul of Shammat. Klorathy says:

> Have you ever – has Shammat ever – asked what would happen if Shammat went to Canopus and said, 'Teach us, we are no longer thieves?' . . . Shammat, it might surprise you to know that you understand more about us than any planet in the Galaxy . . . There are many ways to the path of the Purpose. When are you going to understand what it is you could be doing? (SA 197–8)

The exchange between Klorathy and Krolgul is indeed startling here (and its apparent outrageousness is emphasized by Incent's recorded protests of horror), as startling as if a Houyhnhnm and a Yahoo got together.

The relation between narrative voices and readers is equally startling on the linguistic level, since much of the text articulates the confrontation between Shammat and Canopus in the battles over and through rhetoric. Alongside the parodies that I have already mentioned are subtler exposures by repetition rather than overt analysis or distortion. Words like *empire, agent, logic,* and *power* appear in every verbal register, in all styles of debate, until the complexity, the contradictions within their potential for meanings, must surely give any alert reader pause. We are not allowed any easy interpretation overall, as the novel ends on a deflationary note with a resigned, far from superhuman, message from Klorathy, *en route* for Shammat: 'Unfortunately I was overoptimistic about poor Incent, who has had a relapse. Convinced that it is his mission to reform Krolgul he . . .' (SA 220). Empires rise and fall, and Klorathy has said (just as Johor said in *Representative*) that Canopus is not invulnerable in this process. The novels of the series continually assert that all powers take part in a dynamic, not static, process, and Canopus is certainly shown to be fallible: its original plans for Shikasta, in the first book of the series, go astray. And, as has been demonstrated, its representatives seem to show a decline in their powers through succeeding generations: Klorathy, the pupil of Johor, is more vulnerable than his master, while Incent, Klorathy's pupil, is more vulnerable still, indeed comically so. And, in view of the

41

reported conversation between Klorathy and Krolgul quoted above, might we remember that *timing* is another keyword throughout *Sentimental Agents*? Might Incent's 'relapse' be a step towards the harmonizing of Canopus and Shammat?

The series Canopus in Argos: Archives explores the outer and inner space of planets, zones, and galactic empires. It would be neat and easy to equate planets with outer, zones with inner space: but where would that leave Planet 8 in *The Making of the Representative*, for instance? The essay on Scott's Antarctic expedition at the end of this fourth book appears to point to a certain kind of interpretation – until we note that Doris Lessing asserts that her reflections on Scott actually inspired the previous work, *The Sirian Experiments*, and not the work on ice, doom, and the oneness of the group in the novel to which the essay is teasingly appended. Let readers interpret for themselves, as the texts insist they do.

By moving into space fiction in these five works, and by maintaining extraterrestrial points of view, Doris Lessing risked her reputation in less 'respectable' areas of fiction and confronted her readers with the potential for defining their own dilemmas less narcissistically than, I would suggest, works of 'realism' tend to do, since the latter allow us more unthinkingly to identify with characters and to 'place' the action. Like Orwell, like the writers of magic realism (and Doris Lessing is the link, through the ways in which fable can be used, in this unlikely pairing), she has never been afraid of stylistic risks or, most productively, of literary mischief, as her exposure, in *The Grass is Singing*, of the use of unspoken pressure in discourses of power proclaimed at the start of her writing career. And, by lending her name and reputation to space fiction, she does not, I would repeat, decline into escapism. She challenges her readers more profoundly in this series than some devotees of their own interpretations of *The Golden Notebook* would allow.

6

Jane Somers and a Return to 'Realism'

But, while Canopus in Argos: Archives was being published, Doris Lessing was involved in a very different enterprise, which demonstrates the validity of an argument put forward by Michel Foucault in his article, 'What is an Author?' (1968). In this article, Foucault explains the importance of author-function, in relation to both texts and ideas generated in society. As regards text, he says:

> Such a name permits one to group together a certain number of texts, define them, differentiate them from and contrast them to others. In addition, it establishes a relationship among the texts . . . The author's name serves to characterize a certain mode of being of discourse: the fact that the discourse has an author's name, that one can say, 'this was written by so-and-so' or 'so-and-so is its author', shows that this discourse is not ordinary everyday speech that merely comes and goes, not something that is immediately consumable. On the contrary, it is a speech that must be received in a certain mode and that in a given culture must receive a certain status. (Foucault, 107)

Certainly the name Doris Lessing carried considerable weight by the 1980s; paperbacks of her more recent novels appeal to one aspect of author-function, its selling power, as they proclaim, for instance, 'Mrs Lessing's most adventurous, imaginative experiment since *The Golden Notebook*' or 'the brilliant new novel by the author of *The Golden Notebook*'. Meanwhile Doris Lessing herself was sending two novels round publishers which were written not under her own name, but as 'Jane Somers'. It was some time before these books were accepted for publication and, when her cover broke, there were a lot of recriminations. But in my view, it is typical of Doris Lessing that she should have been drawn to think about the role of her own name in her continuing success with publishers and readership, and then to wonder what impact books without the benefit of her name might have.

The first novel, *The Diary of a Good Neighbour* (1983), tells the story of a middle-class, middle-aged woman who makes friends with an old working-class woman, lonely, living in squalor, but full of vitality. The second novel, *If the Old Could . . .* (1984), remains with the middle-class protagonist of the first book as she reviews her marriage, after the death of her husband, through the insights of a profound love-affair. Both novels explore, in a return to the realistic mode of *The Summer before the Dark*, ways in which education of the sensibilities and social conscience can occur in old- and middle-age. The writing is as vivid and perceptive as in any of Doris Lessing's other works. Here, for instance, in *The Diary of a Good Neighbour*, is how the successful journalist, Janna, first meets old Maudie in the chemist's:

> I saw an old witch. I was staring at this old creature and thought, a witch. It was because I had spent all day on a feature, Stereotypes of Women, Then and Now. *Then* not exactly specified, late Victorian, the gracious lady, the mother of many, the invalid maiden aunt, the New Woman, missionary wife, and so on. I had about forty photographs and sketches to choose from. Among them, a witch, but I had discarded her. But here she was, beside me, in the chemist's. A tiny bent-over woman, with a nose nearly meeting her chin, in black heavy dusty clothes, and something not far off a bonnet. (*DGN* 12)

This fantasy impression (which incidentally reveals a good deal about the journal that Janna works for, and the compartmentalizing which she is accustomed to, a compartmentalizing which current society encourages, as it too tends to 'discard' certain unwelcome aspects of old age) is soon blotted out by reality and by growing insight, as Janna is slowly drawn into the appallingly deprived and squalid life of Maudie, who is too old and ill to cope. The friendship between this unlikely pair is sensitively charted, with Janna gradually learning the language of poverty, isolation, and despairing courage, seeing through the stereotype to the individual, and learning to love and respect what she finds, despite filth, stench, incontinence, senility.

In 1985 Doris Lessing published the next novel under her own name, *The Good Terrorist*, another work in realistic mode, but with strong fabular elements. It pursues the fates of a group of people rejected by and rejecting society, dividing the blame for their macabre, misconceived tragedy between establishment and professional revolutionary groups. Here Doris Lessing shows her usual courageous willingness to grapple with what society would prefer to ignore, and to show compassion in what might be termed contemporary taboo areas. And the novel had a mixed reception. For instance, in the *New York Times*, Denis Donaghue wrote that it was 'bound to give comfort to the middle classes, if only because their enemies, Alice and her friends, are so ludicrously inept'. A strange reading, one might be forgiven for thinking, given that the group's ineptitude results in the deaths of a number of innocent people, and that their pronouncements echo many of the blood-chillingly simplistic tirades of organizations like *Class War*.

It seems to me that *The Good Terrorist* weaves together all kinds of issues. What happens when the individual loses its allegiance to any community, loses a sense of group responsibility; what happens when quotations from Marx and Lenin, say, are simply treated out of context and without thought; what happens when genuine causes for social concern (for example, nuclear arms, Northern Ireland, threats to the environment, housing scandals, breakdown in democratic debate – all of which crop up in *The Good Terrorist*) are adopted by disturbed individuals, not for the sake of the cause, but to work off some personal grudge or psychological problem?

And indeed the central characters in *The Good Terrorist* at heart embrace anarchy rather than anarchism or socialism. Only Alice succeeds for a time in uniting their very separate, self-oriented concerns into some kind of collective; and her motivation stems more from a deep-seated need for a stable home and family than from genuine commitment to socialism. And the house where the group is squatting is very important to the plot. Earlier books alert us to the importance of buildings as images for social order or disorder. From the vision of the city in the first 'Martha Quest' book through to the various settlements, homes, and rooms in Canopus in Argos: Archives, not to mention the 'Jane Somers' flats and bed-sits (or indeed the family home in Doris Lessing's most recent novel, *The Fifth Child* (1988)), buildings are eloquent images for ideas. And the house in *The Good Terrorist* is no exception. It is undoubtedly a house built for the 'bourgeoisie', but it is also a house scheduled for demolition by the council, which has then left it and its neighbour empty for far too long.

When Alice first moves in, we read of the 'rubbish' piled high in the garden and the 'shit' stinking in pails on the second floor. Alice is appalled by the fact that council *workmen* (because they are workers, they should have foreseen squatters) have put cement in the lavatories. Her ideas of revolution are visionary and euphoric, her only skills on the level of everyday life, she cannot accept the gap between the two, and the inevitable confusion this causes is released in bouts of hysteria. The house is a central image for the ultimate weakness of the group. Animal functions are taken care of – the rubbish is removed, the shit buried (and throughout the book the words *rubbish* and *shit* are continually used as terms for what the collective wants to do away with in society), the kitchen works. But wrong-headedness, mirrored by the house's rotten roof-beams, typifies the group as collective and as individuals. Their only form of union is their opposition to all kinds of authority, all forms of discipline, if these fail to meet their idiosyncratic needs.

All members of the group are wrong-headed, but Alice is peculiarly so, because of her inconsistencies. She genuinely cares for individuals, has a genuine sense of the importance of the group, and yet she can be cruel and divisive. In theory she is a socialist, but she has never read Marx or Lenin, treating their names like holy images. When she uses words to express her socialism, she lapses into jargon and stock platitudes (ironically, her mother was an 'intellectual' socialist of working-class background, who appeared to brush aside the growing Alice for the sake of the 'cause' and has lost faith by the time we meet her). In Alice, the need for love and the hatred bred of rejections have produced a naïve but emotional form of ideological commitment: she is the perennial 'baby', although aged 36.

All the central characters are shown up as wreckers of causes, because they merely use the causes for their own titillation and, like children, abandon them if they suffer a set-back. At the same time, Doris Lessing insistently shows this childishness as the product of society. Her vision is never less than compassionate (in a way familiar from the attitude to the infant terrorizers in *Memoirs*), never divorces ideology from circumstance, always implicitly and sometimes explicitly takes the system to task for these irresponsible, stunted children which it has helped to create. The central characters are both victims of the society which has damaged them, leaving them as alienated individualists with no clear idea of how to operate collectively, and wreckers of the causes they espouse, since each of them is seeking to satisfy his or her own needs rather than to serve a cause.

And in the background there are the professional terrorists, who are represented as facelessly as the system of local government and Welfare State. They do not spell out aims or intentions; we cannot even tell who is representing what cause. The professionals give no guide-lines to Alice or her group on how to lead useful 'revolutionary' lives; they make no more attempt to educate and integrate these maimed and confused anarchists than the capitalist society which is ostensibly the common enemy. And here there are illuminating parallels with *The Fifth Child*: in this novel, when Harriet takes her monstrous fifth child, Ben, to the doctor's, to school, and so on, everyone tries to insist on his normality. He must fit in and be seen to fit in or be rejected and, when he rejects in turn, justify being rejected (the syndrome Foucault traces in *Madness and Civilisation, Discipline and Punish*). Only those already outside the conventions of various kinds of community can and do accept Ben, who is both threat and victim, and whose deficiencies, as they have to be termed in the context of contemporary society, reach back to the roots of human society and act as a fabular, dystopic challenge to all concepts of the progress of civilization.

Alice in *The Good Terrorist* has affinities with Ben, although her role as misfit does not have the biological implication of his (it is suggested that Ben is the result of a regressive gene from a far from Golden Age). Alice, like Ben, is both threat and victim, but, unlike Ben (since her alienation is not sustained by his biological integrity, peculiar though it may be to him alone), she finally cracks. It is, I think, with a sense of inevitability that we watch Alice, at the critical moment before the disastrous bombing, both try to get help from the Samaritans so as to save lives and blurt out as an afterthought her assertion that the bombing is the work of the IRA. Where Ben cuts loose from family and society, followed by a group who need him, Alice chooses, alone and deprived of all other needs, to remain in the house she has so passionately fought for. It is Alice who will meet the professionals alone at a point when we cannot but see that her wits have utterly deserted her; it is Alice who thinks vaguely that she might hide from them in the attic, be 'safe' there (and where, she has forgotten, she first noted that the beams were rotten).

And she is alone. The rest of the 'collective' has dispersed; and here again there are links with *The Fifth Child*. Just as in *The Good*

Terrorist the collective is ironized out of existence even before it disperses, so, in *The Fifth Child*, the family, idealized and romanticized by its members and friends at the beginning of the work, disintegrates under Ben's failure to observe the rules of belonging on which it depends. In the end only the mother remains, and then, as she comes to accept, only as an observer of Ben's destiny that rejects all family bonds because, in every aspect of his being, he does not belong.

Both *The Good Terrorist* and *The Fifth Child* expose society's complacency and demonstrate the fragility of so many of the ways by which society, family, the 'professionals', define themselves when confronted by elements which refuse, inherently, to accept and abide by the rules implicit in such definitions. David, Ben's father, can only cope by seeing the child, not as his, but as an alien from the past, although Harriet, Ben's mother, has the courage to see that 'all those different people who lived on earth once – they must be in us somewhere' (*FC* 114). Ben none the less destroys the family as a group before taking to a nomadic existence beyond the bounds of society's constraints, while Alice's group explodes a highly destructive bomb before she herself retreats into a world of madness which can be her only refuge. Like William Golding (in, for example, *Lord of the Flies, Darkness Visible*), Doris Lessing has the courage to face the monsters within society, ignoring society's unvoiced self-censorship, challenging its discourses in ways which are often, quite literally, unacceptable to that society. In the end, Harriet does not blame Ben, even though she cannot accept him: she can sympathize with his loneliness because she has sacrificed all her family to it. Doris Lessing's novels do not take sides, do not manipulate us into blaming Harriet or Ben, Alice or her group of misfits. They simply show us, with appalling clarity, the elements within society, within family, that are the seeds of their destruction.

7

Language and the Short Story

I have so far concentrated almost exclusively on Doris Lessing's novels. But throughout her career she has never ceased to write short stories. She is, like D. H. Lawrence or Katherine Mansfield, supremely gifted as a short-story writer, never wasting a word, and equally at home presenting precisely crafted plot, incident, meditation, or reflective description. It is hardly surprising that the novels often pick up and expand on material used in short stories, just as the novels, as I have tried to show, set up dialogues with each other. What the short stories give is an opportunity to dwell on details of the awesome range of Doris Lessing's narrative skills. And they also demonstrate her command of language. I make this point since, over the years, a number of critics have accused her of stylistic clumsiness. But such an accusation fails to take account of what her narrative voices do with their clumsinesses. Jargon, cliché, platitude abound, to be sure, but that is because we live in a world dominated by jargon, cliché, and platitude. And Doris Lessing is not the writer to duck out of such failures of communication if they need exposing and, in the best teaching method, parodied, mirrored, shown in action and in their effects. We have seen such treatment of language throughout the novels, exposing discourses of power, for instance, wherever they occur: in magazines, in political and bureaucratic pronouncements, in definitions of madness, and so on. Sometimes language itself is the issue, as in *The Sentimental Agents*, sometimes it is the vehicle; but it is always crafted, and, if there is clumsiness, discord, it is because, as in the language of Thomas Hardy, there is clumsiness, discord, to expose and express.

The awareness of what happens when inappropriate Bakhtinian languages are used in the wrong contexts, with their alien vocabulary, is elegantly demonstrated, for instance, in the story 'The

Old Chief Mshlanga', where the narrator recalls how, as a child growing up on an African farm,

> Her books held tales of alien fairies, her rivers ran slow and peaceful, and she knew the shape of the leaves of an ash or an oak, the names of the little creatures that lived in English streams, when the words 'the veld' meant strangeness, though she could remember nothing else.
> Because of this, for many years, it was the veld that seemed unreal; the sun was a foreign sun, and the wind spoke a strange language.
> The black people on the farm were as remote as the trees and the rocks. They were an amorphous black mass, mingling and thinning and massing like tadpoles, faceless, who existed merely to serve, to say 'Yes, Baas', take their money and go. (*CAS* 13–14)

But then a little older and out with her gun and her dogs, she meets an old man with two young ones in attendance, coming along a path, and learns that he is a chief, while the words used to describe the encounter reveal a new language to the narrator:

> A Chief! I thought, understanding the pride that made the old man stand before me like an equal – more than an equal, for he showed courtesy and I showed none.
> The old man spoke again, wearing dignity like an inherited garment, still standing ten paces off, flanked by his entourage, not looking at me (that would have been rude) . . . (*CAS* 16)

And gradually, after seeing the old man a number of times, the narrator begins to change, as is demonstrated in the changing terms of reference:

> Soon I carried a gun in a different spirit; I used it for shooting food and not to give me confidence. And now the dogs learned better manners. When I saw a native approaching, we offered and took greetings; and slowly that other landscape in my mind faded, and my feet struck directly on the African soil, and I saw the shapes of tree and hill clearly, and the black people moved back, as it were, out of my life: it was as if I stood aside to watch a slow intimate dance of landscape and men, a very old dance, whose steps I could not learn. (*CAS* 17)

This is a large insight, sketched with deft economy and an ear for changes in Bakhtinian languages. 'The Sun between their Feet' offers a quite different scale of perception, as the narrator watches two tiny dung beetles trying to roll their ball of dung up a rock, and compares what she sees, the immensity of the effort (is that where the boulder-pushers of *The Golden Notebook* came from?), with what 'the book' on natural history says they do; there is a splendid contradiction of the book's assured, confidently instructive voice, as it distils its information, by the frenzied activity and endless defeats of the beetles as they struggle with their ball in real life. Their daylong efforts, the narrator's attempt to help them at one point (only to have them go back to the bottom of the slope again since they must clearly finish their task themselves), are told in absorbing detail, until the sheer wonderment at the beetles' dedication obliterates the 'facts' so coolly described in 'the book'. And the narrator is driven to reflect: 'Sacred beetles, these, the sacred beetles of the Egyptians, holding the symbol of the sun between their busy stupid feet. Busy, silly beetles, mothering their ball of dung again and again up a mountain when a few minutes march to one side would take them clear of it' (*MTW* 64). Yet in the end it is the narrator who is driven away by the storm which has washed the beetles off the rock and, as she runs, she thinks of the beetles, 'lying under the precipice up which, tomorrow, after the rain had stopped, and the cattle had come grazing, and the sun had come out, they would again labour and heave a fresh ball of dung' (*MTW* 66). Here the language of heroism is dissected, shown up as folly, and then reinstated as a tribute to persistence in the face of failure. The story is a delicately elegant achievement.

In the latest collection, *London Observed: Stories and Sketches* (published in 1992; and also under the title *The Real Thing* in the States), Doris Lessing has lost none of her skills. The first story, 'Debbie and Julie', is a sensitive depiction of tragedy, where a schoolgirl ends up giving birth in a derelict shed, and abandons her baby in a telephone kiosk. This tale, in a few pages, evokes the claustrophobic sterility of a petit-bourgeois home ruled by convention that pregnant Julie flees, and also the love of promiscuous Debbie, who understands Julie's need and yet, as Julie realizes, 'it was not she, Julie, who had earned five months of Debbie's love and protection, it was pregnant Julie, helpless and alone' (*LO* 20). The tale ends in bitter irony, as Julie's father lets out the one skeleton in a dreary family cupboard, the acceptance of an aunt's love-child, only for Julie to see that the aunt had achieved that acceptance by belatedly submitting to acceptable, dreary conformity. This is a richly complex little tale of a freedom, a very contemporary freedom, won at frightening cost.

The range of stories in this collection is as exciting as that found in any of Doris Lessing's earlier works. At the far end of the spectrum from 'Debbie and Julie', for instance, is a four-page sketch, 'Principles', where a Ford Escort (female driver) and a red van (male ditto) have blocked a narrow Hampstead street because neither is prepared to reverse. The farcical developments as more and more vehicles are brought to a standstill has all the immediacy of commentary on the manoeuvres involved in a sporting event, as here:

> The man in the lorry was shouting that everything was the fault of the woman driver up in front, but the Toyota girl wasn't going to have that. She said nothing, but sat smiling, a tight angry little smile. The man in the lorry jumped down, shook his fist at the Toyota, then – for good measure – at me, and strode smartly up past us both and past the Golf, and reached the two vehicles standing nose to nose. He had not been able to see from the cab of the lorry that the red van – male – was more in the wrong than the Escort. He shouted a little at the woman in the Escort, just for the look of the thing . . . (LO 61)

And so on. At the end of the sketch, the car and van still confront each other, blocking the way.

8

Non-Fiction

This same capacity for modulating from tragedy to comedy, for shifting perspective from story-telling to minutely observed description, from narrative to reflection, can also be found in Doris Lessing's non-fiction. There is no sharp demarcation line between fact and fiction in her work, any more than in the writings of D. H. Lawrence or George Orwell. I have already shown the links between *A Ripple from the Storm* and *Going Home*, and there are clear affinities between *The Diary of a Good Neighbour*, the early chapters of *The Four-Gated City*, and a work presented as non-fiction, *In Pursuit of the English*, (1960). I use the phrase 'presented as non-fiction' deliberately, because the book has an elegant shaping of theme, a mischievously witty series of conversations and precise placing of climaxes, more commonly associated with fiction; and, in fact, the blurring of the boundaries between fact and fiction within a text, as here, is a way of getting close to the truth of a situation, as Doris Lessing has frequently demonstrated in her novels.

Set in the first year of Doris Lessing's arrival in England, *In Pursuit of the English* looks penetratingly, affectionately, and humorously at her first rooms in an eccentric working-class boarding house, or rather, house with rooms to let. The characters are vividly drawn: a spiv, a couple on the make, a shop-girl, a prostitute, and so on. The book captures and celebrates a certain element in the London of 1950, violent and capable of moments of vitality and warmth, without much sense of the outside world. There are moments, well placed, which give food for thought, as when Rose, the determinedly apolitical shop-assistant, talks about the presentation of the working class and its accents in British films:

> Them film people just put it in to be clever, like the barrow-boys, it makes the upper-class people laugh. They think of the working-class as dragged

up. Dragged up and ignorant and talking vulgar-ugly . . . And the bloody British can keep their films. I don't mind when they have a film about rich people. You can go and have a nice sit-down and take the weight off your feet and think: I wish that was me. But when they make pictures for people to laugh at, then they've had me and my money. I'll keep my money for the Americans. You don't take them serious, and anyway they don't laugh at people with different voices in America. That's because America is all foreigners, the way I look at it, and they can't all laugh at each other, can they? (PE 112–13)

This is funny and also makes a point; and, being presented within a dialogue between 'Doris' and Rose, there is no narrational comment. Later in the book, the old people who continue to live as sitting tenants in the house are depicted, and their determination, squalor, and savagery are vividly portrayed with a humour and compassion which will be echoed in *The Diary of a Good Neighbour*, where the colourful language of Flo, the landlady, will be merged with their obstinacy and wretched living conditions to create the old woman Maudie.

But Doris Lessing does not only rework her raw material; she revisits and reviews it. In *A Small Personal Voice: Essays, Reviews, Interviews*, edited by Paul Schlueter (1974), there is an affectionate essay on her father, and the dreamer he was. He is not so very different from Martha Quest's father, a man given to insights and depression, a loser in practical matters. Eleven years later, she wrote two articles for *Granta* ('Impertinent Daughters' and 'My Mother's Life, Part Two') in which she looks back on her unhappy relationship with her mother and puts the record straight, showing her in youth as a feminist, highly successful as a nurse, a fine pianist, a woman who loved the social whirl – only to end up on a poor African farm, miles from the nearest neighbour. Doris Lessing shows the psychological inevitability of what happens to her mother in her frustration; but she also shows her generosity and honesty, just as she did, more obliquely, in *The Memoirs of a Survivor*, when the narrator visits and comes to understand what is presented as Emily's mother in the world of inner space. At the end of 'Impertinent Daughters', Doris Lessing admits:

Writing about my mother is difficult. I keep coming up against barriers, and they are not much different now from what they were then. She paralysed me as a child by the anger and pity I felt. Now only pity is left, but it still makes it hard to write about her. What an awful life she had, my poor mother! But it was certainly no worse than my father's, and that is the point: he was equipped by nature for hard times, and she was not. He may have been a damaged, an increasingly sick man; she was strong and full of vitality. But I am not as sorry for him as I am for her. She never understood what was happening to her. (*ID* 68)

This capacity for compassion and understanding, even when she is affected most nearly, equips Doris Lessing for writing compellingly about humanitarian causes. She has written often and movingly about southern Africa, but she took on a very different and difficult subject when she went to Pakistan with a group representing the charity Afghan Relief, publishing her reactions to the visit in *The Wind Blows away our Words* in 1987. The book offers a view of the resistance to the Russian invasion of Afghanistan, a consideration of the role of women in Afghan society, and a brilliant description of the conditions under which refugees were living. She examines racism from different angles; political and national prejudices; sexism; propaganda, and so on. But she also knows that to start a work of this kind with a straight plunge into fact is likely to alienate those very readers who are not yet wedded to the cause, since there are now so many causes urgently clamouring for our attention. So the first part of her book is utterly unexpected, following as it does a dedication 'to the gallant people of Afghanistan'. It is a witty retelling of part of the story of Troy, told as from Helen's and Cassandra's point of view; and they in turn (like Anna and Molly in *The Golden Notebook*) can be taken as two aspects of the same person; or indeed each of them can be seen as an individualization of a multitude (with haunting echoes of *The Making of the Representative*). As Doris Lessing says:

These days Cassandra is not a divinely inspired sybil, or old women weeping disregarded in corners, or old soldiers who lost everything in a war. Cassandra is a shout of warning coming from everywhere, particularly from scientists whose function it is to know what is likely to happen, from people everywhere who concern themselves with public opinion, anyone who thinks at all. You could say the whole world has become Cassandra, since there can be no one left who does not see disasters ahead. (*WBW* 16)

And not only are people merged into a single representative; events too merge. Doris Lessing points out, chillingly, 'In fact Troy had already been built and then sacked and burned to the ground six times. (Homer's was the seventh Troy). Helen does not know this repeated calamity has been blurred to make one, generic calamity' (*WBW* 27). This evocation of the Troy legend to show individuals trapped in the generic calamity of the twentieth-century world is a bold innovation in the art of contextualization, showing, as it does, myth and legend in the making. Doris Lessing will not let us treat the Afghan war as a localized conflict. Her questions spill over into Pakistan, her anger and compassion reach out to many issues that she does not intend her readers to ignore. Some critics have protested at her digressions; but the whole book is a refusal to compartmentalize. Doris Lessing exposes the discourses emanating from war and interrogates them, concluding that:

> We consider some forms of murder worse than others . . . Six million Jews, one million gypsies – that makes seven million [of the 12 million estimated to have died in Hitler's concentration camps], and leaves five million. Who were they? . . . We ourselves are the prisoners of these numbers, these figures, the statistics – the millions; and millions upon millions. Is it possible that our careless, our casual, use of these 'millions' is one of the reasons for brutality, for cruelty?
>
> Writing this I have been haunted by some words of the Russian poet Osip Mandelstam who died in the Gulag:
>> 'and only my own kind will kill me.' (*WBW* 170–2)

We are uncomfortingly reminded that not only the victims, the events, the prophets of doom merge into each other, but so do the destroyers. Demolishing the rhetoric of disengagement, Doris Lessing confronts us with the language of involvement.

And so she does in *African Laughter: Four Visits to Zimbabwe* (1992). This is a wonderfully rich book. Doris Lessing has said that it gave her great trouble in the writing, that she had in fact to rewrite it. And this is hardly surprising in view of its complexity. The title suggests that it covers just the four visits made since 1982; but in fact, we are given a great deal more than that. Past speaks to present, black speaks to white, political promises confront what happens in practice, granite reveals its properties, the bush is filled once more with wildlife and then emptied, to reveal incipient desert or the Kariba lake. Some reviewers have grumbled, predictably, wanting their own versions of then and now. Why is she well disposed to the whites, ask some? But the whites in these pages speak with many voices, as do the blacks, some generous and big-minded, some bigoted and deaf to argument, some self-seeking and blind to their fellows. Others ask, why does she dare to criticize so young a regime? But again, the narrative, and the people she meets, speak with many voices, praising achievements, discussing shortcomings, always pointing to the dynamics of development. Pros and cons are debated by many people, black and white, throughout the work. Doris Lessing is too clear-eyed about what went wrong with Marxism under Stalin to insult her readers with a book based on political correctness; she offers us a portrait of a much-loved country and its people, warts and all, and brings it alive.

She does not offer us long sweeps of narrative as she did in, for example, *Going Home*. Instead, she builds on the technique used in *Shikasta*, giving short pieces under headings, which can be read as continuities or absorbed in isolation, while the headings point us to the central concern of each section. At no point is she playing the part of the infallible reporter; she is Doris Lessing, going back to the place she grew up in, not wanting to visit the site of the old family farm for fear of 'tampering with my myth, the bush I was brought up in, the old house built of earth and grass, the lands around the hill, the animals, the birds. Myth does not mean something untrue, but a concentration of truth' (*AL* 35). But on the next visit she does dare to go back, and then travels on to a much-loved spot, slowly disappearing under a new reservoir, where she remembers watching, with her brother, a troop of baboons, many years before,

> guarded by a big male who kept his eye on us, warning his people with grunts and barks if we moved carelessly. We watched them all go down to the river to drink, perhaps fifty or so of them, the little ones on their mothers' backs. Then they merged back into the hills, the big male going last, sending us across the river a final admonishing bark.
>
> All that land is going under the water. Going, going . . .
>
> Well, what of it, says the voice of commonsense – mine, at least sometimes. This happened in Europe centuries ago. (*AL* 318-9)

But nostalgia is only a small part of Doris Lessing's profound and intricate dialogues. Elsewhere she deplores those whites who ignore the poverty of many Africans, while showing 'the tenderest solicitude' to threatened animals. And she (who has told us of many lifts she has given when driving herself) tells of the whites who take her on a drive and refuse, despite her furious protests, to offer a lift to a pregnant black woman. But the incident is then placed in a larger context, in retrospect, following the strategy employed in *The Wind Blows away our Words*:

> Since then an obvious thought has added itself to those already in my mind which I might have had before: no one was likely to give this woman a lift . . . everywhere in the world this peasant woman, with one (or two) babies inside her, one on her back, one or two clutched by the hand, is slowly walking up a mountain, and we can be sure that few people see her. (*AL* 137)

This passage makes no excuses for the whites in that particular car, but as always Doris Lessing is not afraid to present an unfashionable truth, exposing the way power, not just race, all too often behaves. It takes a lot of courage to utter this kind of simple truth, just as it takes a lot of courage, for instance, to do what a group of women are doing in Zimbabwe. Doris Lessing accompanies them on a trip to invite other African women to contribute to a book, 'stories, poems, songs, jokes, articles, it doesn't matter what'. The meeting, she says, reminds her of

> stories about early days in the Russian Revolution, when idealism still governed events . . . One difference: there is not one word about politics. Not one slogan. No rhetoric.
>
> These women are not only being asked to take control of their lives, without submitting to men, but to overcome reluctance to talk to women who might come from an area a hundred miles or so from their own. Here, we are cutting across tribal and clan divisions . . . This women's book is subversive in ways immediately evident to the women themselves – and the local officials, who are sitting at the back of the room, watching. (*AL* 240)

The scheme is not being monitored in order to be suppressed; on the contrary, it is gradually winning government support and co-operation. This detail is one of many which makes the book an optimistic one, by and large. Optimism does not, of course, imply euphoria, but Doris Lessing never loses her faith in human nature, while always keeping faith with it.

In April 1992 a conference was held at Rutgers University on the subject of 'Intellectual and Social Change in Central and Eastern Europe', and the proceedings were published in a Special Issue of the *Partisan Review* (fall, 1992). Doris Lessing was one of the participants, giving a paper entitled 'Unexamined Mental Attitudes Left Behind by Communism'. In the spirit of *The Good Terrorist*, she is not attacking socialism as such, but the way it was practised in the Soviet Union, the way the Soviet model was all too often romanticized by socialists in the West, and the way the jargon of political correctness has insidiously invaded the English language. When discussing this last point, she argues that Communist jargon has left a legacy of 'dead and empty' language which is 'still to be found in some areas of academia and particularly in some areas of sociology, psychology, and some literary criticism' (*UMA* 722), and she deplores the fact that so many students from developing countries 'will believe that this is the English language and that this is how they should write and speak it' (*UMA* 723). She goes on to deplore the idea that writers are in some circles obliged to write to some political formula (and her argument echoes what she said, for instance, in the preface to *The Golden Notebook*): 'If a writer writes truthfully out of individual experience then what is written inevitably speaks for other people. For thousands of years storytellers have taken for granted that their experiences must be general. It never occurred to them that it is possible to divorce oneself from life . . .' (*UMA* 724).

She also deplores what she sees as another legacy of Communism: that, again in some circles, books must have a message, be about some social or political issue, or, in other words, are expected to behave like the heirs of socialist realism, 'and yet the history of storytelling, of literature, tells us that there has never been a story that does not illuminate human experience in one way or another' (*UMA* 725). She argues that 'habits of mind' have been absorbed from Communism, often unconsciously, and adds: 'It troubles me that political correctness does not seem to know what its exemplars and predecessors are; it troubles me a good deal more that they may know and do not care' (*UMA* 726). This is a powerful point (although it must be said that political correctness in practice, if not as a phrase, goes back centuries before Communism, as Janáček's opera, *The Adventures of Mr Brouček*, mischievously demonstrates, locating it in the tyrannies of church and aristocracy). In her paper Doris Lessing goes on to point to the excitement of revolution, the romanticization of causes far from home alongside denigration of one's own culture, the romanticization of certain kinds of violence – and the way in which the legacy of Communism has damaged 'the left-wing, the social, even liberal movements of Europe . . . because the progressive imagination was captured by the Soviet experience' (*UMA* 729).

Looking at the fate of Western socialism since the end of Russian Communism, she maintains:

> we did not have to identify with the Soviet Union, with its seventy-odd years of logic-chopping, of idiotic rhetoric, brutality, concentration camps, pogroms against the Jews. Again and again, failure. And, from our point of view, most important, the thousand mind-wriggling ways of defending failure. I think the history of Europe would have been very different. Socialism would not now be so discredited, and above all, our minds would not automatically fall into the habit of 'capitalism or socialism'. (*UMA* 729)

Her conclusion is 'that until we know the patterns that dominate our thinking and can recognize them in the various forms they emerge in, we shall be helpless and without real choice. We need to learn to watch our minds, our behaviour. We need to do some rethinking. It is a time, I think, for definitions' (*UMA* 730).

I have quoted from this article at some length as it ties in with much that has emerged in this discussion of Doris Lessing's work. She has, as I have tried to show, a keen ear for the abuse of language and a sure sense of how to expose the folly of words through words themselves, while never losing her own sensitivity to what language can achieve, as she shows in so many short stories, so many descriptions of the veld, so many aphorisms. This sense of language is a sign too of her ironic awareness of ideological simplifications; even when a member of a Communist group, she could pinpoint and demonstrate with wry economy the gap between political word and meaning, as she could in other areas, such as sex, race, or literary criticism. And she is always true to her story-telling tradition. She writes out of personal experience – although one might be forgiven for seeing her personal experience as so rich and varied that she inevitably appears to offer a message, in that she does indeed perceive 'the patterns that dominate our thinking and can recognize them in the various forms they emerge in' (*UMA* 730), and can therefore offer us a chance to do the same throughout her work.

So I mean to end where I began, as it seems to me that Bakhtin does indeed offer the most fitting final comment on Doris Lessing's work so far, since she, of all living novelists, most fully explores the 'diversity of individual voices' which he describes as 'the internal stratification of any single national language', with its 'social dialects, characteristic group behavior, professional jargons, generic languages, languages of generations and age groups, tendentious languages, languages of the authorities, of various circles and of passing fashions, languages that serve the specific sociopolitical purposes of the day, even of the hour . . .'. No one is able to explore these languages, which Bakhtin considers to be 'the indispensable prerequisite for the novel' (Bakhtin, 263), better than Doris Lessing, and we do well to mark, quite literally, her words. As she says, 'We need to learn to watch our minds, our behaviour. We need to do some rethinking. It is a time . . . for definitions' (*UMA* 730).

Select Bibliography

WORKS BY DORIS LESSING

Doris Lessing's works present bibliographical complexities, as she has worked with a number of publishing houses over the years on both sides of the Atlantic. The majority of her work is readily available in paperback, but she has appeared under a wide range of imprints (in England, for example, under Triad, Picador, Panther, Penguin). This bibliography is necessarily highly selective when referring to paperbacks. (It should be noted that Paladin and those Lessing titles appearing in Grafton are gradually being subsumed under the HarperCollins imprint, Flamingo.)

Books, plays, and collections

The Grass is Singing (London: Joseph; New York: Crowell, 1950; paperback edn., London: Collins (Paladin), 1989).

This was the Old Chief's Country (short stories) (London: Joseph, 1951; New York: Crowell, 1952).

Martha Quest (Children of Violence, vol. i) (London: Joseph, 1952; New York: Simon and Schuster, 1964; paperback edn., London: Collins (Paladin), 1990).

Five: Short Novels (London: Joseph, 1953; paperback edn., London: Collins (Paladin), 1991).

A Proper Marriage (Children of Violence, vol. ii) (London: Joseph, 1954; New York: Simon and Schuster, 1964; paperback edn., London: Collins (Paladin), 1990).

Retreat to Innocence (novel, now out of print) (London: Joseph, 1956).

Going Home (London: Joseph, 1957; paperback edn., London: HarperCollins (Flamingo), with added afterwords, 1992).

The Habit of Loving (short stories) (London: MacGibbon and Kee; New York: Crowell, 1957; paperback edn., London: Grafton, 1985).

A Ripple from the Storm (Children of Violence, vol. iii) (London: Joseph, 1958; New York: Simon and Schuster, 1966; paperback edn., London: Collins (Paladin), 1990).

Each his own Wilderness (play), in E. Martin Browne (ed.), *New English*

Dramatists 1 (London: Penguin, 1959); Willis Hall (ed.), *The Long and the Short and the Tall and Each his own Wilderness* (London: Penguin, 1968).

Fourteen Poems (now out of print) (Northwood, Middlesex: Scorpion, 1959).

In Pursuit of the English (London: MacGibbon and Kee, 1960; paperback edn., London: HarperCollins (Flamingo), 1993).

Play with a Tiger (play) (London: Joseph, 1962); in J. M. Charlton (ed.), *Plays of the Sixties*, vol. i (London: Pan, 1966); V. Sullivan and J. Hatch (eds.), *Plays by and about Women* (New York: Random, 1973).

The Golden Notebook (London: Joseph; New York: Simon and Schuster, 1962; paperback edn., London: Collins (Paladin), 1989).

A Man and Two Women (short stories) (London: MacGibbon and Kee; New York: Simon and Schuster, 1963; paperback edn., London: Collins (Paladin), 1992).

African Stories (London: Joseph, 1964; New York: Simon and Schuster, 1965, see below, *Collected African Stories*).

Landlocked (Children of Violence, vol. iv) (London: MacGibbon and Kee, 1965; New York: Simon and Schuster, 1966; paperback edn., London: Collins (Paladin), 1990).

The Black Madonna (short stories) (London: Collins (Paladin), 1992).

Winter in July (short stories) (London: HarperCollins (Flamingo), 1993).

Particularly Cats (autobiographical) (London: Joseph, 1967).

Nine African Stories (London: Longman, 1968).

The Four-Gated City (Children of Violence, vol. v) (London: MacGibbon and Kee; New York: Knopf, 1969; paperback edn., London: Collins (Paladin), 1990).

Briefing for a Descent into Hell (London: Cape; New York: Knopf, 1971; paperback edn., London: Grafton, 1972).

The Story of a Non-Marrying Man and Other Stories (London: Cape, 1972; paperback edn., London: Collins (Paladin), 1990); US edn. published as *The Temptation of Jack Orkney and Other Stories* (New York: Knopf, 1972).

Collected African Stories, i. *This was the Old Chief's Country*; ii. *The Sun between their Feet* (London: Joseph, 1973; paperback edn., London: Collins (Paladin), 1992).

The Singing Door (one-act play), in A. Durband (ed.), *Second Playbill Two* (London: Hutchinson, 1973).

The Summer before the Dark (London: Cape; New York: Knopf, 1973; paperback edn., London: Collins (Paladin), 1990).

The Memoirs of a Survivor (London: Cape; New York: Knopf, 1974; paperback edn., London: Pan (Picador), 1976).

A Small Personal Voice: Essays, Reviews, Interviews, ed. with an introduction by P. Schlueter (New York: Knopf, 1974).

Collected Stories, i. *To Room Nineteen*; ii. *The Temptation of Jack Orkney* (London:

Cape, 1978; paperback edn., London: Grafton, 1979); US edn. published as *Stories* (New York: Knopf, 1978).

Re: Colonised Planet 5, Shikasta (Canopus in Argos: Archives, vol. i.) (London: Cape; New York: Knopf, 1979; paperback edn., London: Grafton, 1981).

The Marriages between Zones Three, Four and Five (Canopus in Argos: Archives, vol. ii.) (London: Cape; New York: Knopf, 1980; paperback edn., London: Grafton, 1981).

The Sirian Experiments (Canopus in Argos: Archives, vol. iii) (London: Cape; New York: Knopf, 1981; paperback edn., London: Grafton, 1982).

The Making of the Representative for Planet 8 (Canopus in Argos: Archives, vol. iv) (London: Cape; New York: Knopf, 1982; paperback edn., London: Grafton, 1983).

Documents Relating to the Sentimental Agents in the Volyen Empire (Canopus in Argos: Archives, vol. v) (London: Cape; New York: Knopf, 1983; paperback edn., London: Grafton, 1985).

The Diary of a Good Neighbour by Jane Somers (London: Joseph; New York: Knopf, 1983).

If the Old Could . . . by Jane Somers (London: Joseph; New York: Knopf, 1984).

The Diaries of Jane Somers (London: Joseph; New York: Vintage, 1984; paperback edn., London: Penguin, 1985).

The Good Terrorist (London: Cape; New York: Knopf, 1985; paperback edn., London: Collins (Paladin), 1990).

The Wind Blows away our Words (London: Pan (Picador), 1987).

The Making of the Representative for Planet 8: An Opera in Three Acts, libretto by Philip Glass and Doris Lessing (based on the novel) (Bryn Mawr: Dunvagen Music Publishers, Inc., 1988).

The Fifth Child (London: Cape; New York: Knopf, 1988; paperback edn., London: Collins (Paladin), 1989).

The Doris Lessing Reader (London: Cape; New York: Knopf, 1989; paperback edn., London: Collins (Paladin), 1991).

London Observed: Stories and Sketches (London: HarperCollins, 1992); US edn. entitled *The Real Thing* (New York: HarperCollins US, 1992).

African Laughter: Four Visits to Zimbabwe (London: HarperCollins; New York: HarperCollins US, 1992).

Prefaces and endnotes

'Author's Notes on Directing this Play' (1963) and 'Postscript' (1972), *Play with a Tiger*.

'Preface' (1973), *This was the Old Chief's Country*; 'Preface' (1973), *The Sun between their Feet*.

'Eleven Years Later' (1967), *Going Home*.

'Afterword', Olive Schreiner, *The Story of an African Farm* (New York: Fawcett

World Library, 1968), repr. in *A Small Personal Voice* and subsequently in *The Doris Lessing Reader*.
'Author's Notes' (1969), *The Four-Gated City*.
'Preface' (1971), *The Golden Notebook*.
'Some Remarks' (1978), *Re: Colonised Planet 5, Shikasta*.
'Preface' (1980), *The Sirian Experiments*.
'Afterword' (1982), *The Making of the Representative for Planet 8*.
'Preface' (1984), *The Diaries of Jane Somers*.
'Preface' (1989), *The Doris Lessing Reader*.

Selected uncollected material

1. There are several uncollected poems, going back as far as 1943 (in *New Rhodesia*, Salisbury). There are also a number of uncollected, early short stories; and one or two plays (including *The Truth about Billy Newton*, first produced at Salisbury Playhouse, Wilts. (1960); then on BBC television (5 June 1961).
2. There are a large number of uncollected articles, including:
    'Ordinary People', *New Statesman*, London, 25 June 1960.
    'The Education of Doris Lessing', *Observer Supplement*, London, 26 Sept. 1971.
    'Impertinent Daughters', *Granta*, Cambridge, 14 (winter, 1984).
    'Unexamined Mental Attitudes Left Behind by Communism', *Partisan Review*, Special Issue (fall, 1992), 722–30.
3. There are several reviews, on books and theatre (including, for instance, 'The Living Past', on performances of Ibsen's *Ghosts* and Brecht's *Mother Courage* (*Observer*, London, 16 Nov. 1958); and 'African Interiors', on Van der Post's *The Heart of the Hunter* (*New Statesman*, London, 27 Oct. 1961).
4. There are a number of forewords and introductions to the works of others, including:
    'Introduction', in A. E. Coppard, *Selected Stories* (London: Cape, 1972).
    'Introduction', in Ramsay Wood, *Kalila and Dimna: Selected Fables of Bidpai* (London: Paladin, 1982).
5. Scripts, broadcasts, and tapes include:
    'Memories of the Vlei', a talk for BBC Radio, London, 15 Aug. 1952.
    'Virginia Woolf', a discussion for 'Bookstand', BBC TV, London, 8 Jan. 1963.
    'Do not Disturb', a TV script for 'Blackmail', ITV, London, 25 Nov. 1966.
    'Doris Lessing Reads her Short Stories', a tape recorded at the Poetry Centre, New York (New York: Jeffrey Norton, 1974).
6. There are a number of uncollected letters to journals and newspapers, such as 'A Plea for the Paperback', *Guardian*, London, 3 July 1972.
7. There are numerous interviews as, for example:

Bergonzi, Bernard, 'In Pursuit of Doris Lessing', *The New York Review of Books*, New York, 11 Feb. 1965.

Langley, L., 'Scenarios of Hell', *Guardian Weekly*, London, 24 Apr. 1971.

Tomalin, Claire, 'Mischief: Why a Famous Novelist Played a Trick on the World', *Sunday Times*, London, 23 Sept. 1984.

BIOGRAPHICAL AND CRITICAL STUDIES

Books

Alexander, M., *Flights from Realism: Themes and Strategies in Postmodernist British and American Fiction* (London: Hodder & Stoughton (Edward Arnold), 1990).

Bakhtin, M. M., *The Dialogic Imagination: Four Essays by M. M. Bakhtin*, ed. M. Holquist, trans. C. Emerson and M. Holquist (Austin: University of Texas Press, 1981).

Bertelsen, E. (ed.), *Doris Lessing* (Southern African Literature Series, 5; Johannesburg: McGraw-Hill Book Company, 1985). This book has a very fine bibliography up to 1984.

Bloom, H., *Doris Lessing* (Modern Critical Views; New York: Chelsea, 1986).

Draine, B., *Substance under Pressure: Artistic Coherence and Evolving Form in the Novels of Doris Lessing* (Madison: University of Wisconsin Press, 1983).

Fishburn, K., *The Unexpected Universe of Doris Lessing: A Study in Narrative Technique* (London: Greenwood, 1985).

—*Doris Lessing: Life, Work, and Criticism* (Authoritative Studies in World Literature; Fredericton, NB: York, 1987).

Foucault, M., *The Foucault Reader*, ed. P. Rabinow (London: Penguin, 1984).

Fullbrook, K., *Free Women: Ethics and Aesthetics in Twentieth-Century Women's Fiction* (Brighton, Sussex: Harvester Wheatsheaf, 1990).

Gardiner, J. K., *Rhys, Stead, Lessing, and the Politics of Empathy* (Everywoman Studies in History, Literature, and Culture; Bloomington, Ind.: Indiana University Press, 1989).

Greene, G., *Changing the Story: Feminist Fiction and the Tradition* (Bloomington, Ind.: Indiana University Press, 1991).

Gurr, A., *Writers in Exile: The Identity of Home in Modern Literature* (Harvester Studies in Contemporary Literature and Culture, 4; Brighton, Sussex: Harvester; Atlantic Highlands: Humanities, 1981).

Hanley, L., *Writing War: Fiction, Gender, and Memory* (Amherst: University of Massachusetts Press, 1991).

Hite, M., *The Other Side of the Story: Structures and Strategies of Contemporary Feminist Narratives* (Ithaca: Cornell University Press, 1989).

Kaplan, C. and Rose, E. C. (eds.), *Doris Lessing: The Alchemy of Survival* (Athens: Ohio University Press, 1988).

—*Approaches to Teaching Lessing's The Golden Notebook* (Approaches to

Teaching World Literature, 23; New York: Modern Language Association of America, 1989).

Kaplan, C., *Sea Changes: Essays on Culture and Feminism* (London: Verso, 1986).

King, J., *Doris Lessing* (Modern Fiction; London: Edward Arnold, 1989).

Knapp, M., *Doris Lessing* (Literature and Life Series, New York: Ungar, 1984).

Laing, R. D., *The Divided Self* (London: Penguin, 1965).

—*The Politics of Experience and The Bird of Paradise* (London: Penguin, 1967).

McNay, L., *Foucault and Feminism* (Oxford: Polity Press, 1992).

Meaney, G. *(Un)like Subjects: Women, Theory, Fiction*, (London: Routledge, 1993).

Pickering, J., *Understanding Doris Lessing* (Understanding Contemporary British Literature; Columbia: University of South Carolina Press, 1990).

Popa, V., *Collected Poems 1943-1976*, trans. Anne Pennington with an introduction by Ted Hughes (Manchester: Carcanet New Press, 1978).

Robinson, S., *Engendering the Subject: Gender and Self-Representation in Contemporary Women's Fiction* (SUNY Series in Feminism; Albany: State University of New York Press, 1991).

Rubenstein, R., *The Novelistic Vision of Doris Lessing: Breaking the Forms of Consciousness* (Chicago: University of Illinois Press, 1979).

Sage, L., *Doris Lessing* (Contemporary Writers; London: Methuen, 1983).

—*Women in the House of Fiction: Post-War Women Novelists* (London: MacMillan, 1992).

Showalter, E., *A Literature of their Own: British Women Novelists from Brontë to Lessing* (Princeton: Princeton University Press, 1977).

Sinfield, A. (ed.), *Society and Literature, 1945–1970* (New York: Holmes & Meier, 1983).

Sprague, C. and Tiger, V. (eds.), *Critical Essays on Doris Lessing*, (Critical Essays on Modern British Literature; Boston: Hall, 1986).

Sprague, C., *In Pursuit of Doris Lessing: Nine Nations Reading* (New York: St Martin's, 1990).

Taylor, J., *Notebooks/Memoirs/Archives: Reading and Rereading Doris Lessing* (Boston: Routledge, 1982).

Whittaker, R., *Doris Lessing* (MacMillan Modern Novelists; London: MacMillan, 1988).

Articles

The *Doris Lessing Newsletter* (now published by the Brooklyn College Press) was founded in the early 1980s, and its articles are generally of a high standard. Articles published in it are not included in the following list, although the journal is recommended.

Agatucci, C., 'Breaking from the Cage of Identity: Doris Lessing and the Diaries of Jane Somers', in J. Morgan, C. T. Hall, and C. L. Snyder (eds), with a foreword by M. Hite, *Redefining Autobiography in Twentieth-Century Women's Fiction: An Essay Collection* (New York: Garland, 1991), 45-56.

Bawer, B., 'Doris Lessing: On the Road to *The Good Terrorist*', *The New Criterion*, Sept. 1985, 4–17.

Fishburn, K., 'Wor(l)ds within Words: Doris Lessing as Meta-Fictionist and Meta-Physician', *Studies in the Novel* (summer, 1988), 186–205.

Hite, M. '(En)Gendering Metafiction: Doris Lessing's Rehearsals for *The Golden Notebook*', *Modern Fiction Studies* (autumn, 1988), 481–500.

Knapp, M., 'Canopuspeak: Doris Lessing's Sentimental Agents and Orwell's 1984', *Neophilologus* (July, 1986), 453–61.

Maslen, E., 'One Man's Tomorrow is Another's Today: The Reader's World and its Impact on Nineteen Eighty-Four', in G. E. Slusser, C. Greenland, and E. S. Rabkin (eds.), *Storm Warnings: Science Fiction Confronts the Future* (Carbondale: Southern Illinois University Press, 1987), 146–58.

Peel, E., 'Utopian Feminism, Skeptical Feminism, and Narrative Energy', in L. F. Jones and S. W. Goodwin (eds.), J. Pfaelzer, (response), J. B. Elshtain (response), *Feminism, Utopia, and Narrative* (Knoxville: University of Tennessee Press, 1990), 34–49.

Sage, L., 'The Available Space', in M. Monteith (ed.), *Women's Writing: A Challenge to Theory* (Brighton, Sussex: Harvester; New York: St Martin's, 1986), 15–33.

Whittaker, R., 'Doris Lessing and the Means of Change', in L. Anderson (ed.), *Plotting Change: Contemporary Women's Fiction* (London: Edward Arnold, 1990), 1–16.

Index